Demonic Vision

*Racial Fantasy
and Southern Fiction*

Alan Henry Rose, 1938 –

Archon Books • 1976

Library of Congress Cataloging in Publication Data

Rose, Alan Henry, 1938-
    Demonic vision.

    Bibliography: p.
    Includes index.
    1. American fiction—Southern States—History and
criticism.   2. Afro-Americans in literature.   3. Indians in
literature.   4. Race problems in literature.   I. Title.
PS261.R55   813'.03   76-12088
ISBN 0-208-01582-5

Contents

Acknowledgements

Professor Terence Martin of Indiana University provided the rigorous advice that gave this book initial shape, and the continuing encouragement that saw it through its long development. The major influence upon the work is his. I wish also to thank Professor Warren French of Indiana University-Purdue University at Indianapolis, and Professors J. Albert Robbins and James H. Justus of Indiana University for their suggestions. Conversations with Professors Robert L. Carringer of the University of Illinois and Robert E. Abrams of the University of Washington played an important role in the ways of thinking of the book. Ms. Maureen A. Kearney provided invaluable help in preparing the manuscript for press. My deepest gratitude is to Dr. Harriet A. Rose, whose contribution to this book in every area far exceeded all reasonable expectations.

Introduction

Produced some fifty years after the Civil War, D. W. Griffith's cinematic portrayal of violent racial hatred in the Reconstruction South, *The Birth of a Nation,* attracted an audience of over two million within six months. The movie was screened before President Wilson and his cabinet, and seen immediately afterward by the Supreme Court and members of Congress. In view of its staggering nationwide reception, together with its uncontested advertising claim to White House endorsement,[1] *The Birth of a Nation* seems almost an official document of America's continuing fear of the black man, and its need to suppress him.

Yet in spite of the notorious melodramatic freedom with which Griffith treated his theme, his racism seems moderate when compared to that in the novel which provided the film much of its compelling plot and characterization, Thomas Dixon, Jr.'s *The Clansman* (1905). Among the episodes omitted from the movie is a crucial one which serves as the turning point of the novel. By identifying the specific Negro rapist of a white Southern girl, Dixon's plantation owners find a focus for their pent-up hatreds, and are galvanized into the organized repressive violence which forms the basis of the Clan. The identification is made through a distortion of reason which shares a long tradition of using scripture, history, and science to prove the black man "naturally" inferior. A white Southern doctor turns optical technology to the uses of racism, asserting "that a microscope of sufficient power will reveal on the retina of [the girl's] dead eyes the image of this

devil as if etched there by fire.'' The doctor finds his image, but the
form it takes lends an unexpected meaning to the apparently casual
diabolical reference: he sees ''the bestial figure of a negro—his
huge black hand plainly defined—the upper part of the face is dim,
as if obscured by a gray mist of dawn—but the massive jaws and
lips are clear.''[2] Like Satan's, the black man's malevolence, writ
as if by fire and merging with the ''gray mist of dawn,'' seems a
first principle.

Underlying the story which gripped the imagination of early
twentieth-century America is a depiction of the Negro drawing on
no less a source than the irresistible fascination with prime evil.
However repugnant it seems, the diabolical racial image central to
The Clansman suggests a way of seeing the black man which
touches many Americans, but largely originates in the South, and
is felt most intensely by Southerners. In the eye of the Southerner,
and in the magnifying vision of his fiction, which—in the words of
Joel Kovel—''goes to the symbolic roots of [Southern] experience, lays them bare and re-creates them anew for us in their
immediate form,''[3] the Negro, and the Indian too, in varying
shades of intensity may take on the shape of the devil. In Southern
fiction, seeing the black man and the red man demonically brings
about a dramatic vitality; the writings tap a profound source of
unconscious energy. But such a dark primordial vision inevitably
provokes the shadow of fear and the impulse toward repression.
The following pages will explore the nature of demonic vision in
the South, and its far-reaching influence upon Southern fiction.

The source of the demonic in white racial fantasies lies in a
particularly destructive psychological process. Kovel explains that
for the white psyche, ''the ego designates the id, which is unseen,
as having the quality that comes from darkness; as being black.
The id, then, is the referent of blackness within the personality;
and the various partial trends within the id, all repressed, make
themselves symbolically realized in the world as the forms of
blackness embodied in the fantasies of race.'' As an id figure for
the white man, the Negro has had projected onto him ''whatever is
forbidden and horrifying in human nature.''[4] As James P. Comer

puts it, "Nobody was more vulnerable to the 'projection of evil' or psychological exploitation than the black man."[5] The Negro has consistently seemed a threat in popular fantasies. The danger may be expressed in terms of turn-of-the-century moralism: " 'A bad Negro is the most horrible human creature upon the earth, . . . the most brutal and merciless'; even ministers or teachers 'are never made cowards by conscience, nor do they suffer the stings of remorse.' " But the harsh racism of the Reconstruction South came closest to the point. For many postbellum Southerners, Negroes were dangerous because they were "wild African savages who lacked internal restraints."[6] Underlying the varying forms of the white racial vision is the apprehension of a figure, representative not of human complexity, but, as Ralph Ellison suggests, symbolic of just one aspect of humanity.[7] Sterling Brown has demonstrated some seven one-dimensional ways the white has seen the Negro.[8] This study deals with a single vision of the black man that has received surprisingly little attention. As an id figure to the white, the black has from earliest times symbolized the most basic fears of uncontrolled disorder, of primordial irrationality. In white racial fantasies, the Negro has often served as "a symbol of instincts run wild."[9]

The white European of course already had a traditional image with which to express the dangers of the uncontrolled id: the devil. "The devil," in C. G. Jung's definition, "is a variant of the 'shadow' archetype, i.e., of the dangerous aspect of the unrecognized dark half of the personality."[10] The two concepts merged with telling ease. Winthrop D. Jordan demonstrates that to the Elizabethan, "the *devil*" was "a mediating term" for the Negro's dominant characteristics, his "barbarity and blackness." There was, according to Jordan, a dramatic "completeness with which English perceptions could integrate [libido] with blackness [and] the devil. . . . These running equations lay embedded at a deep and almost inaccessible level of Elizabethan culture." Harry Levin also notes the ancient diabolical connotations of blackness.[11] It seems clear that in 1619 a profoundly influential association was implanted in the American South. In that year the first slaves arrived, and, in the manner described by Sir Thomas Herbert, appeared "in colour . . . little other than Devils incarnate."[12]

Yet a second coincidence complicated the white's equation of the Negro with the devil. America contained a figure who also in color and savagery seemed expressive of primordial abandon: the Indian. As Roy Harvey Pearce suggests, to the English voyager the Indian seemed more animal than rational, and his barbaric irrationality too was attributed to the devil: "Satan had possessed the Indian until he had become virtually a beast." John Smith made an early connection between red man and devil: "Their chiefe God they worship is the Divell." Other Elizabethans saw the Indian as "the servants of sinne and slaves of the divell." But the Indian's diabolical quality held the greatest significance for early Americans. It was the Puritans, with their highly defined concept of God and Satan, who formalized for America the vision of the Indian as Satan realized in actuality. "The Puritan," as Pearce says, "discovered in the Indians themselves evidence of a Satanic opposition to the very principle of divinity." "Wherever the Indian opposed the Puritan, there Satan opposed God."[13] The association of the Negro with bestial irrationality, of the Indian with similarly profound disorder, the view that the disruptive quality of the two races stemmed from Satan, and the consequent blurring together of Negro and Indian as both agents of the devil formed an equation that is fundamental to the American psyche.

This white racial vision was shaped by the formal imagery already associated with the archetype of the devil. In varying degrees, in the expressions of such fantasies, Negroes and Indians take on diabolical form: they display a serpentine quality, acquire horns, seem hoofed. Sometimes demonic attributes belonging to other malevolent supernatural beings haunting the unconscious merged with the diabolical imagery. Black and red men may reveal fangs like vampires, or be dwarfed with disproportionately long arms and carry cudgels, like leprechauns. But most crucially, the Negro or Indian may appear in imagery which traditionally has been most closely connected with the devil: that of fire. Dramatically, in racial fantasies, the black or red man appears in intimate relation to flames viewed as the fires of hell. A Negro displaying a body "like a frog's," "immensely long arms," and "short bow legs," appears in John T. Trowbridge's 1863 novel, *Cudjo's Cave,* and outlines one form of this association. Amidst a conflagration, the black man, who had "belonged to a tribe of African fire-worshippers, from whom he had been stolen in his youth," is seen as "a wild human figure making fantastic gestures, and prostrating itself towards the burning forests." The fire is his "God! . . . comin' fur burn up de white folks, and set de brack man free!" Again suggesting the devilish source of the relationship in the white author's imagination, another black man summons a fire's fury with a diabolical invocation: "Burn, ye debil! K-r-r-r! sputter! snap! git mad, why don't ye?"[14] A little-discussed meaning of lynching, the ritual expressive of the darkest Southern racial attitudes, illustrates the depth of the black's relationship with fire in the white imagination. In the South, Negroes sometimes were burnt, not hanged. In one such instance in 1921, "There was a wild scramble of the mob to secure [the black's] bones as souvenirs." As a reporter from the *Memphis Press* put it, "To read the details of lynching is to be reminded of the torture of the Middle Ages."[15] When desperate, the South sought to combat its racial fear by exorcising the basic manifestation of the black man's diabolism. Resurrecting an ancient ritual, the Southerner used fire to fight hell-fire.

In Southern literature, the unconscious force conveyed by the Negro or Indian grows in proportion to his expression of demonic characteristics. According to Jung, apparently lesser projections of the unrecognized dark half of the personality may produce a matrix of manifestations classifiable under the rubric of the primitive "power-concept." The id figure may then seem to convey "the idea of . . . bodily strength, fertility, magic, influence, power."[16] For some time, literary critics have detected varying combinations of these qualities in fictional portraits of the Negro and Indian. Daniel G. Hoffman, for example, has seen Nigger Jim in *Huckleberry Finn* as a magus, in contact with nature's secrets. Others, Kenneth S. Lynn among them, allude to a darker expression of the black man's subjective role in Southern fiction, to momentary glimpses of a "dreadful, half-savage beast, with a smile on his face and murder in his heart." And Leslie A. Fiedler has touched on the devilish nature of the Southern racial vision, finding it, in Edgar Allan Poe's *The Narrative of Arthur Gordon Pym,* the depiction of "a world in which the primitive may save or destroy, but remains always brutal and amoral, from any Christian point of view—diabolic."[17] Critics, however, have not as yet dealt with the implications for fictional expression of the dark figure's demonic associations in the Southern imagination. For, as Maud Bodkin explains, the devil archetype may introduce into literature a power which is "unlimited, formless, negative," "a force . . . threatening the hero's values both from within and from without— exciting in him an emotion that has a 'numinous' element in its horrified resistance or surrender."[18] Seen most demonically, the black or red man conveys in Southern fiction the full disruptive content of the devil archetype. At such moments the expression of the dark figure may threaten ordered form and, in reaction, induce the emergence of techniques necessary to restore stability to the fictional narrative.

To the Southerner, nervously living among dark peoples, politically beleaguered, acknowledging the full depth of racial fear obviously was anathema. The relationship between Southern fiction and demonic vision in varying ways reflected the responses made by Southern culture to its apprehension of racial danger. In the 1830s the forms by which the South defended against the threat of the Negro and Indian crystallized concurrently. Perfect safety was thought of primarily in terms of separation. In the case of the Indian, for whom slavery had not paid off, separation became feasible. Through Removal, the South simply rid itself of its red men. Between 1830 and 1840 virtually all the Cherokees, the Choctaws, and the Creeks were transported westward.[19] By the late years of the 1830s when this study begins its treatment of the red man in Southern literature, the Indian danger in the South seemed conclusively buried, and "the Indian everywhere was known to be one of the lost." A defensive wish had become a reality. Northerners eagerly endorsed the situation, making the Indian, in Pearce's words, an abstract metaphor for the savage past, "a scholarly field in himself, just like a dead language." In Northern literature, distant Indian savagism was "sentimentally or melodramatically ennobled out of existence."[20] Southerners too exploited the Indian in literature, but, in a land still facing a racial threat, he served a radically different function. Without posing a real danger of its own, Indian savagery came to seem an effective metaphor for the expression of repressed fears of Negro violence. Through the medium of the underlying equation of black and red diabolism, in the period from Removal to the Civil War, and in varying degrees afterward, the expression of the Indian paradoxically mushroomed in the intensity of its demonic content.

Thoughts of separation from the Negro also preyed on Southerners; as Lawrence J. Friedman points out, before the Civil War "Thomas Jefferson, James Madison, Henry Clay, and other prestigious leaders had often championed the proposal"[21] to colonize the black man. But the wish for racial isolation in the South was not so easily enacted with the Negro as with the Indian. The South had established a society intrinsically involving menial black labor; as Charles G. Sellers, Jr. puts it, "The individual planter's economic stake in slavery was a stubborn and perhaps insurmountable obstacle to change."[22] Nat Turner's rebellion in August, 1831, and the formalization of abolitionist sentiment in organs such as William Lloyd Garrison's *The Liberator*, forced the Southerner into open debate about slavery. The discussion occurred in the General Assembly of Virginia in the Winter of 1831-1832. Its outcome was a close but decisive vote in favor of retaining the institution. That resolution, combined with the new cotton economics, confirmed the role of slavery in the South, and frustrated any realistic hope for the mass removal of the black race as well as the red.

Wanting distance, and after 1832 finding instead a heightened intimacy, the Southerner evolved a substitute means to defend against his fears of the Negro. With the Negro as with the Indian, abstraction underlay the white racial response; through dehumanization the Southerner enhanced his sense of control over the black man.[23] The impulse was expressed through a sharply increased emphasis upon racial stereotypes—"images," as Catherine Juanita Starke defines them—"that whites could accept, reject, or ignore without qualm of conscience or depth of emotional response."[24] Easily most effective among antebellum racial stereotypes was the Sambo, a totally harmless black figure, with which the Southerner opposed his intuition of the Negro threat. Stanley M. Elkins provides a complete definition of this dehumanized image:

> Sambo, the typical plantation slave, was docile but irresponsible, loyal but lazy, humble but chronically given to lying and stealing; his behavior was full of infantile silliness and his talk inflated with childish exaggeration. His relationship with his master was one of utter dependence and childlike attachment: it was indeed this child-like quality that was the very key to his being. Although the merest hint of Sambo's "manhood" might fill the Southern breast with scorn, the child, "in his place," could be both exasperating and lovable.[25]

The Sambo stereotype formed the cornerstone of the South's proslavery argument. As the South marshalled public expression to provide the appearance of unanimity in defense of slavery, the belief in a contented slave population gave credibility to the vision which justified the "neo-feudal insistence on the necessity of subordination and inequality in society," the image of the happy plantation. Yet this seductive idea of celestial order made real was rent with private confessions of fear, for, as Sellers demonstrates, "The surface unanimity enforced on the South . . . concealed a persistent hostility to slavery."[26] The resultant cultural tension influenced antebellum fiction. While producing fiction primarily intended to defend the slaveocracy, the Southern novelist, William R. Taylor suggests, sometimes was subject to a conflicting impulse to see his society darkly, "a marked tendency to view the Tidewater planter critically or satirically, and to see his world as . . . threatened by disruptive forces in its very midst." It is questionable that much of the Southerner's racial introspection found expression in Southern fiction in the period just before the Civil War. Even the greatest disruptions in the literary plantation at that time are usually viewed, with the overt optimism that Robert William Fogel and Stanley L. Engerman demonstrate was a characteristic of the Southern economy in the 1850s, as temporary misfortunes in the process of correction.[27] But without doubt in the years immediately following the Great Debate the South was still influenced by its time of self-examination. In the fiction of the middle 1830s the otherwise effective Sambo stereotype did indeed sometimes falter, and behind it could be caught glimpses of the figure underlying Southern racial fears, the malevolent black demon.

The Civil War marked a watershed in the treatment of the black man in Southern fiction. Without slavery, the Southerner lost the institutional basis for his motivating utopian illusion, but the lure of the illusion remained. Southern fiction continued to portray the happy plantation, but without a corresponding reality. Guy A. Cardwell defines the effects of the new situation upon the central image of the plantation house: "The polemic, linearly logical elements decrease; the affective, nostalgic, and dreamlike elements increase; and the image of the house—taking on indefiniteness, whispering of profundities—becomes less metaphoric [in terms of its relation to structural social elements] and more symbolic."[28] The expression of the Negro in popular fiction after the war revealed a similar transformation, becoming even less realistic, displaying the release from logic associated with dream, without political controls seeming more than ever a symbol of the white's desperation in the face of his continuing racial fears.

Unstabilized in this manner, in the years after the war the great part of Southern expression about the Negro split into two extreme fantasies of racial control. In one, the new plantation tradition, centering on the nostalgic vision of Thomas Nelson Page, "the literary plantation," as Taylor says, became "an idyllic sanctuary, a kind of sunny Shangri-la, into which the cares of the world rarely intruded."[29] In this hopelessly utopian vision, racial relations normally displayed a totally placid unreality, based on the ultimate development of the Sambo stereotype. In addition to his other characteristics, the Sambo in Page's novels reveals "courage, fortitude, and self-sacrifice," as Hugh M. Gloster puts it, "in relieving the destitution and distress of the Southern aristocracy during and after the war."

The other extreme reversed the utopian dream, making it into a nightmare of "uncompromising Negrophobia and unrivaled vituperation."[30] Led by the novels of Thomas Dixon, Jr., this literary mode sought to focus white fears onto a black figure, and through scapegoating him, purge the community of its malaise. In contrast to the Sambo, these Negroes, in Starke's words, were "vilified as prurient beasts . . . who, because they defied prescribed rituals of race relations, deserved their punishment of torture and mutilation."[31] In its frenzy to portray the Negro as malevolent, this fiction, illogical in the deepest sense, sometimes gives a dramatically full expression to demonic vision.

Each of these postbellum modes of racism was an assertion "with new vehemence" of racial attitudes which stemmed from the antebellum proslavery imagination, and which had been expressed in a somewhat less extreme form in pre-Civil War fiction.[32] In this study, sufficient examples will be presented from the earlier fiction to justify avoiding the redundance of discussing similar modes of racial expression in the later popular statements. But in addition to the two extremes of racism, the destruction of institutionalized slavery in the South made possible a third manner of treating the Negro in Southern fiction which will be dealt with extensively. With his imagination freed from the enervating obligation to endorse an untenable social system, the serious Southern writer was able to turn to a treatment of the Negro's complex meaning for the white. In their contribution to the Southern "paradox," contradictory racial attitudes have helped form "the materials for a literary expression," as C. Hugh Holman maintains, "uniquely powerful in our time."[33] Yet, for much of the greatest Southern fiction, the racial paradox has taken on a form sometimes subtly, sometimes dramatically reflecting the old, dark vision of the black man. In varying ways, the Southern author has confronted a painful irony: how to view objectively, humanely, a black figure which still involuntarily stirs the deepest psychological fears of disorder. This tension contributes to the tragic stature of much of the fiction of Mark Twain and William Faulkner. Elucidating the profound role of demonic vision in the Southern imagination provides an understanding of this influential dimension in major Southern fiction.

This study spans over a century of Southern writing. During that time the expression of demonic vision underwent many modifications. But it was not until the 1930s that the demonic image began to reflect the seeds of a qualitative shift in Southern racial attitudes. The Depression, Nancy M. Tischler points out, brought an end to the domestic intimacy traditional in the Southern white's relationship with the Negro: "The breaking down of the old easy-going but ruinous relationships of the Southern farm has come close to making meaningless clichés of much of what the Southern white man thought and said about the Negro." In the 1930s the Southerner began to see the black man "more often as an economic and social victim. . . . Fired from industry like white men, or driven off the land like white men, Negroes began to look like depressed humans, not members of a peculiar alien species."[34]

World War Two, with its massive diversion of public attitudes to nondomestic concerns, seems a dividing line between the racial reassessments emerging in the 1930s, and the optimistic certainties which crystallized in the 1950s. In the positive postwar context, the white's sense of the Negro's and Indian's dark power has been expressed more through admiration than fear. The cult of the primitive has focused on the black man, and somewhat later on the red man; they have "taken on," as Tischler says in the case of the Negro, self-conscious "symbolic implications: serving as . . . primordial love, . . . as the dark unknown in man's heart and soul."[35] Such treatment often seems exploitative: since the 1950s the dark figure sometimes represents an unconscious power which now receded, no longer threatening, the white author longs once again to experience. Most important, without fear, the white

Southern author is finally free to explore the complex humanity of the Negro and Indian. In recent Southern fiction the dark figure has gained markedly in the fullness of his characterization. But in the last two decades racial expression in Southern fiction largely has lost its demonic vision.

Chapter One

Blackness in the Fantastic World of Old Southwestern Humor

Old Southwestern humor, comprised of short stories and tall tales written largely before the Civil War and most frequently in Tennessee, Alabama, Georgia, Mississippi, and Louisiana, constitutes one of America's most uninhibited modes of fiction. As Walter Blair describes the Southwestern tales, they were "local, authentic, detailed, zestful; they were distinctly masculine, and they dealt largely with the lower classes."[1] According to Arlin Turner, Southwestern humor's particular expressiveness stems from its unconventionality:

> That neither the writers nor the readers of this homely humor considered it literature can be easily demonstrated. And the fact that it originated and existed on a sub-literary level is of very great importance. . . . Thus liberated in considerable degree from the restraints of polite literature, from sentimentality and imitativeness and false elegance, this humor was free to incorporate a realism of materials and language unthinkable in the accepted literary mode of the time.[2]

Unconventionality still further increased the dimensions of expression in Southwestern humor. As Turner suggests, "One consequence of this greater freedom, accentuated at times by a deliberate rebelliousness, . . . was an audacity of conception and with it a richness of imagery which has given us our nearest approach to indigenous fable and a native mythology."[3] This unique variant of local color realism exhibited the capacity to move, with apparent ease,"from the actual toward the fabulous."⁴

apparent ease,"from the actual toward the fabulous." [4]
Southwestern humor also displays a complexity which further contributes to its unique place among the expressive modes of its age. With its potential for depicting disorder, it expresses the violence which was integral to Southwestern frontier society. But the Southwestern humorist was ordinarily a professional man. As Kenneth S. Lynn describes him, he was "a lawyer or a newspaperman, usually, although sometimes a doctor or an actor. He was actively interested in politics. . . . He was well educated. . . . Wherever he had been born, and a few were of Northern origin, the ideal humorist was a Southern patriot. . . . Above all, he was a conservative." [5] His interests coincided with those of the South's stable middle classes; they required portraying the region as an ordered and self-restrained society. Southwestern humor satisfied both poles of the Southern imagination; it implied order as well as describing violence through the use of an effective narrative strategy, the framework technique. The framework establishes a definitive distance between the self-controlled, gentlemanly narrative voice and the violent content of the tale. In Blair's words:

> The circumstances of the telling of the tale were set forth, often with appreciative detail. . . . Then the teller of the tale would be described. . . . Then, in the words of the narrator thus introduced, the tale itself—a reported oral yarn—would be presented. . . . The story itself moved rapidly through its big scene or scenes to its conclusion. At the end, the fireside scene of the opening paragraphs might again receive attention. [6]

In this manner the framework provides an effective temporal spacing; often the tale is set conclusively in the past, and its vanished violence contrasts sharply with the tranquil present. Further, the technique makes possible the transformation of violence into play. "It helped to remove the happenings described by the tale-teller from the realm of harassing reality, to render them less disturbing, more amusing. Recounted in the atmosphere of the quiet, peaceful fireside, even the most harrowing episodes of a frontier tale might become comic."[7] As Lynn points out, "By containing their stories within a frame, the humorists . . . assured their conservative readers of something they had to believe in before they could find such humor amusing, namely, that the Gentleman [narrator] was as completely in control of the situation he described as he was of himself."[8]

Spanning much of the range of regional experience, Southwestern humor depicts the relentless violence of hunters, fighters, and squatters with consistent narrative aplomb. Even describing heroic figures such as Davy Crockett and immortal game like the Big Bear of Arkansas, the tall tale maintains a tranquil perspective while through its capacity for "fable" offering an extensive vision of the Southern imagination. But in dealing with the Negro and Indian, Southwestern humor's capacity for fable created a profoundly ambivalent situation. If it were to share the same expressive freedom with which other archetypal figures were portrayed, the image of the Negro or Indian too would swiftly move from realism to fantasy in the tall tale. Yet the racial image contained compellingly powerful subjective associations, the expression of which was taboo in the South. In the next chapter, the effects this situation had upon the treatment of the Indian will be discussed. With the Negro, one response of the humorist was simply to censor the depiction of the black man from his work: Negroes appear in Southwestern tales with an infrequency far out of proportion to their place in Southern life. Another was to employ stereotypes to mask the racial content. Such restrictive techniques are jarringly out of place in this fiction. The choice facing the antebellum Southern humorist was clear: in some way repress the image of the Negro, or through the customary abandon of the tall tale risk the introduction of an unconscious disorder so extensive as to unsettle narrative perspective and transform Southwestern fantasy into an unrestrained expression of the irrational demonic vision.

The Southern humorist normally opted for repression. As James H. Penrod points out, either the humorists "displayed reticence to treat the Negro at all," or "they assumed a defensive attitude" based upon stereotype.[9] The black stereotype usually serves a simple narrative purpose: it places the Negro in a conventionally stable, inferior relationship with the white protagonist, and, drawing upon the sentimentalized Southern illusion of devotion between slave and master, it establishes his harmless benevolence. The description of the Negro in John S. Robb's "The Pre-emption Right," collected in *Streaks of Squatter Life* (1846), exemplifies the typical use of black stereotype: the hero's

> only companion [was] a negro slave, who was at once his master's attendant and friend. Kelsy and the negro had been raised together, and from association, although so opposite their positions, had imbibed a lasting affection for each other,—each would have freely shed blood in the other's defence. The bonds of servitude were, consequently, moulded into links of friendship and affection.[10]

The development of racial description in a short sketch from Augustus Baldwin Longstreet's *Georgia Scenes* (1835), however, demonstrates the possibility for greater complexity in the use of the black stereotype. In "The Mother and Her Child," as in many of his tales, Longstreet is satirizing an aspect of white manners, "exhibiting one of the peculiarities of the age,"[11] mocking the "gibberish" used with infants. In this case a very unpleasant white mother, "Mrs. Slang," is trying to quiet her baby, whose crying she insistently blames on the child's black nurse, Rose. The interest of the tale lies not so much in the dialogue used with the infant, but in Longstreet's portrayal of the relationship between the two women. At first their association is described with the author's characteristic objectivity. It is cruelly depersonalized. The white subjects the black to continual vilification and beating, coolly adminstered without even the excuse of passion: in Mrs. Slang's blows "there seemed to be no anger mixed at all" (116). The black has been rendered passive by white domination: "Rose received [her beating] *as a matter of course*, without even changing countenance under it" (116). The ugly story of slavery seems expressed in Longstreet's italics.

But this antebellum author's objectivity toward the Negro had its limits. Toward the end of the sketch Longstreet seems compelled to recant the implicit condemnation of the white and compassion for the slave. Mrs. Slang, for all of her inhumanity toward the Negro, is partly redeemed by her relationship with her child: repeatedly she is shown in images of motherhood, suckling and soothing her infant. The point of view about the black in turn becomes hostile. Mrs. Slang throws one of her more figurative threats at her slave: "If you say *'Miss Nancy's bureau'* to me again, I'll stuff Miss Nancy's bureau down your throat, you little lying slut" (119). Rose makes no response, and the author tells us why: "Here Rose was reduced to a *non plus;* for, upon the peril of having a bureau stuffed down her throat, she dare not repeat the oft-told tale" (119). Longstreet has concluded his story with an exercise in racial dehumanization which considerably surpasses the crude techniques practiced by his white heroine. He has applied to the black one of the most insidious racial stereotypes, that based upon the white's denial of the black's capacity for human reason, his "comic" inability to distinguish between the figurative and the literal. It is a measure of the importance attached to reestablishing conventional antebellum racial attitudes that in order to portray the black in this reassuring stereotype Longstreet sacrifices narrative consistency in his tale, abandoning his rigorously detached satire for the sake of an intrusive conjectural slur on the nature of the black intellect.

In unsally demanding situations the use of stereotype could become almost baroquely elaborate. Such an instance occurs in "Samuel Hele, Esq.," a sketch collected in Joseph G. Baldwin's *The Flush Times of Alabama and Mississippi* (1853). Baldwin, a Southern lawyer, makes use of courtroom tactics to apply a twist to the traditional defensive use of stereotype. He appropriates his opponent's stereotypes of racism in the South for an aggressive defense, concealing Southern attitudes toward the Negro behind a grotesque version of Northern abolitionist clichés, particularly the exaggerations "in a very popular fiction, or rather book of fictions" by "Mrs. Harriet S———."[12] Specifically, the tale revolves about the attempt of a Southern spokesman, Hele, to drive away a meddling figure of Northern conscience, Miss Charity Woodey, with a parody of her "prejudices" (291). How the concept is executed can be seen in this one example. Miss Woodey questions, "But, Mr. Hele,—do tell me,—do they *now* part the young children from their mothers—poor things?" (300). Hele in turn spins a tall tale of Southern inhumanity:

> There was a great feud between the planters on this side of Sanotchie, and those on the other side, growing out of the treatment of negro children. Those who sold them off charged the other siders with inhumanity, in drowning theirs, like blind puppies, in the creek; which was resented a good deal at the time, and the accusers denounced as abolitionists. I did hear of one of them, Judge Duck Swinger, feeding his nigger dogs on the young varmints, as he called them. (300)

The technique does effectively block our view of Southern racial attitudes; by the end of this antebellum tale, unique in that it purports to deal with the abuses of slavery, we know nothing specific whatever of the Southerner's thoughts about the Negro. But the very elaboration in this tale leads to a hint of the reason for the defensive urgency. In preparing for his attack, Hele follows a friend's injunction: "Don't spare brush or blacking, but paint the whole community so black, that the Devil himself might sit for the picture" (293). The metaphor of brush and blacking suggests the blinding purpose of the narrative irony, but in equating total blackness with the devil it also, surely with an unintentional irony, draws its very form from the same unconscious diabolical associations of the black man which it attempts to deny.

While metaphoric slips such as Baldwin's hint at the existence of repressed racial associations, the use of black stereotypes normally served as an effective shield against further expression. Even as tensions in the South neared the breaking point with the approach of the Civil War and, as Lynn points out, "the Southwestern humorists were less and less able to control ugly realities by means of [sentimental] myth,"[13] the image of the Negro is still constrained in Southwestern humor. All of the Southerner's regional affiliations demanded that the tensions implicit in the racial question be concealed. Consequently, some influence transcending cultural inhibitions was necessary before the fear and violence which underlay the antebellum vision of the Negro could find expression. Full depiction of the black man in the pre-Civil War South demanded both a sensitivity to the region's cultural forces and a freedom from its restraints upon their depiction. Among antebellum authors, this condition occurred most dramatically in the work of Henry Clay Lewis, who wrote under the pseudonym of Madison Tensas, the Louisiana Swamp Doctor.

Although one of the lesser known of the Old Southwestern humorists, Henry Clay Lewis's tales of medical school in mid nineteenth-century Kentucky and of doctoring in the Louisiana bayous have received considerable recognition. Franklin J. Meine included one of Lewis's tales in his pioneering *Tall Tales of the Southwest* (1930). In *Native American Humor* (1937), Blair placed the Louisiana Swamp Doctor stories among the foremost Old Southwestern fiction. Lewis's tales were reprinted frequently in his own time, notably in T. C. Haliburton's *Traits of American Humor* (1852). As his biographer, John Q. Anderson maintains, most of Lewis's stories were ''well within the mainstream of frontier humor. . . . [They] attempted to portray as accurately as possible the peculiarities of character, attitude, and atmosphere of a specific region or locality.''[14] But, as his collectors realized, Lewis also had the capacity to invest his traditional Southern subject matter, the drunken Indians, itinerant preachers, Virginia aristocrats, bear hunters, and squatters with an imaginative vitality which sometimes gives them a dimension beyond the limits of local color realism. In Lewis's tales realism, as it does in the best of Southwestern humor, carries the potential for intuitive regional fable.

While Lewis's affiliations clearly lay with the South, prompting him to spend his entire life there, to favor Whig politics, and when he could, to keep a Negro body servant, Lewis was a Southerner only by adoption. He was the son of David and Rachel Salomon

Lewis, a Jewish family who claimed ties with Benjamin Disraeli. As a Jew in the antebellum South, Lewis was something of an outsider. At the same time he adopted antebellum Southern values, he was inherently distanced from them. As Anderson suggests, "Lewis's not belonging in the society to which he aspired made him a shrewder observer than most of the lesser humorists of his time" (69). In other words, many of the restraints upon expressing regional taboos were less meaningful to Lewis and tended less to cloud his fiction. One of the inhibitions Lewis did not fully share with his fellow Southwestern humorists was that upon the expression of the Negro. Lewis was one of the few Southern humorists to treat the black man in his fiction extensively and often without stereotype.

The specific characteristics of Lewis's personality compounded the effects of his independence from conventional antebellum inhibitions. An extraordinarily unsettled childhood—in which Lewis lost his mother at six, was abandoned by his father, forced by ill-treatment from one brother to stow away on a river steamer, led by another brother's bankruptcy to work in the cotton fields— seems to have made him seriously unstable. As a doctor, Lewis's instability is legendary; according to Anderson, there is a "story still current in Madison Parish that he was a carefree, reckless, and hot-blooded young man" (52), a "local tradition that Lewis was a reckless young man given to taking chances" (57). When practicing medicine in Richmond, Louisiana, Lewis was convicted of assault and battery; the court record reads: "The State vs Henry C. Lewis: For assault & battery. This case was taken up to be tried—the Defendant plead guilty" (51). Lewis's lack of self-control sometimes may have reached dimensions resembling schizophrenia. Violence in his fiction attains monumental proportions. Moreover, again and again Lewis's darker autobiographical tales give evidence of a blurring of primary psychological distinctions, momentary failures of the capacity to demarcate the boundaries of the self, as in this frenzied outcry in the midst of a medical school brawl: "I had finished giving a lick all round and could hardly keep from pitching into the mirror to whip my reflection, I wanted a fight so badly'' (87).

The form of Lewis's tales also may have been influenced by the disorder of his personality, since it does not share the stability customary in Southwestern humor. As has been discussed, normally the humorist distinguished carefully among himself, his narrator, and the violent material he described. These distinctions were essential to the effective use of the framework technique. In Lewis's case the lines of separation among author, narrator, and persona are obscure. Lewis is a young swamp doctor, recently graduated from medical school; his narrator is a somewhat older swamp doctor, describing the experience of a young swamp doctor from medical school through practice in the bayous. Anderson points out how closely allied Lewis's writing is with his life. The stories are all either fully or partly autobiographical. One result of the blurring of narrative distinctions is the unusually intimate subjective tone of the tales; Lewis's stories are punctuated with emotional outcries, personal confidences, searches for meaning. With the narrowing of narrative distance also came a weakening of narrative control. As do the other humorists, Lewis extensively relies upon the framework to contain the violence he treats. But for Lewis the framework is not always effective. At times, in some of the more ghastly tales, the appearance of temporal separation provided by the framework fades, and, as the sense of the rising violence in which the persona is involved becomes immediate, the author is driven to jarringly abrupt and unreasonable endings in order to place his subject material back in safe perspective.

Instability in narrative control created an explosive situation when combined with Lewis's uninhibited approach to racial description. With the Negro, Lewis was treating material which conveyed a far greater content of disorder than that encountered in his nonracial subjects. Not distinguishing between subject matter, Lewis employed his especially unrestrained descriptive style with the black man, often stressing data which was totally repressed by other humorists. As in Lewis's other tales, the sense of violence in the racial stories becomes quite vivid, as the framework perspective blurs. Yet with the narrowing of narrative distance, an additional dimension of meaning emerges in the violence of these racial sketches. Again and again, the persona displays surprise at an inexplicable, deeply felt influence exercised upon him by the black figure. The expression of such intuitions about the Negro's profoundly irrational characteristics triggers a disruptive spiral in Lewis's narrative, introducing an additional component of disorder which in turn leads to a more abandoned subjective depiction of the black man. This unstable situation takes the capacity for fantasy fundamental in Southwestern humor to an unduplicated extent, and consequently produces an incomparable vision of the Negro's demonic role. But unchecked, the spiral also holds the potential for an ultimate destruction of narrative form commensurate with the limitless irrationality conveyed through the dark image that the tales express.

Racial treatments in Lewis's fiction display a progression of irrationality, reaching a crescendo of disordered fantasy in the tale written shortly before his death, appropriately titled "A Struggle for Life." In the story, "The Curious Widow," several factors limit the Negro's disruptive influence. Primarily, the narrative depicts a passive black figure; this tale of medical school days involves only the face sliced from a dissecting room subject, the corpse of a Negro murderer. It is diabolical enough: "Every feature was deformed and unnatural; a horrible harelip, the cleft extending half way up his nose externally, and a pair of tushes projecting from his upper jaw" (117). But the object lacks the full import of blackness; its owner "was one of that peculiar class called albinos or white Negroes" (117). Moreover, the narrative directs the destructive associations of the face away from the persona. It is used by the persona to frighten the landlady of his boarding house, to retaliate against her for prying through his belongings. This factor, together with the temporal distance of the anecdote in the Swamp Doctor narrator's history—it occurs early in his medical school career, "during my first course of lectures" (116)—lends the framework separation a special effectiveness.

Yet, once the face is separated from the Negro's corpse, the

persona's first action implies the force of its subjective connec-
tions. He compulsively separates himself from it, hiding it beneath
multiple layers of concealing material: "Having procured a yard
of oilcloth, we sewed it to the face and then rolled it carefully up;
tying this securely, we next enveloped it in a number of wrappers,
fastening each separately" (117). The tactic is of course intended
to block the racial object from the person's sight. Vision, however,
is precisely the area where the Negro's unconscious associations
are most actively perceived. Concealed even further, the face still
influences vision. Indeed, in spite of the figure's apparent passivity, in this area it manifests a powerful force: "I endeavored to
sleep; but that hideous face, which we had locked securely in a
trunk, kept staring at me through its many envelopes" (118). Its
disruptive effects upon the persona are marked; he becomes
"nervous and irritated" (118). In Lewis's racial fiction, such a
state of emotional agitation may signal the start of the characteristic spiral of disorganization. In this tale, though, the narrative
distance is reasserted; the persona with a telling ferocity redefines
his intent to direct the disorder away from himself: "My heart, at
this last reflection, became immediately barred to the softening
influences, . . . and I determined in all hostility to *face* her [to use
the face against her]" (118).

From this point through the denouement, the persona remains
entirely an observer to the destructive effects of the racial
encounter. He successfully tempts the widow to open the sinister
package. As she does so, the extent of the subjective dimensions of
its contents is implied, for the narrator suddenly intrudes to discuss
the widow's later death, and relates this "grandest and most awful
mystery of our nature" (119) to the opening of "the last envelope
of the mysterious package" (119). Her final portrayal does suggest
if not death, then a radically destructive disorganization of the self.
About to complete the unwrapping, she seems distorted by gro-
tesquely distended organs of sight, as if her personality had
become dominated by the approaching racial vision: "There she
stood with spectacles buried so deeply 'neath her brows as almost

to appear a portion of her visage'' (120). As she uncovers the object, viewing ''its awful hideousness upon her extended palm—the fiendish tushes protruding from the parted lips—still wearing the agony of the death second—and the eyes enclosed in their circle of red'' (120), the widow appears entirely overwhelmed by her vision. She ''gazed upon its awfulness in silence as if her eyes were riveted to it forever'' (120). The ''hellish countenance'' (120) finally seems totally to disorient consciousness: the widow ''broke into a low laugh. . . . Her laughter was becoming hysterical. We spoke to her—shook her by the shoulder—but still she laughed on, increasing in vehemence and intensity. . . . [Her laughter grew] fiercer, faster, shriller than before'' (120-21). The persona, using medical rhetoric for authority, defines the effects of demonic vision: ''She is gone demented'' (121).

With the narrative depicting such profound irrationality, disorder again edges to dominate the tale. The widow's hysteria attracts a mob: ''In rushed the crowd—a full charge for the room'' (121). But at this critical point the effects of a stable narrative form tell, for ''ere they had time to . . . make a demonstration'' (121), the widow's hysteria is suddenly cut off. The humorous perspective is reasserted in a manner which, if somewhat unlikely, effectively transforms the disorder into joke. The widow is made to give an explanation of her frenzy which redefines the meaning of the racial encounter and relieves it of all its threatening associations:

> The widow ceased her laughter and putting on an expression of the most supreme contempt coolly remarked: ''Excuse me, gentlemen, if I have caused you any inconvenience by my unusual conduct. I was just *smiling aloud* to think what fools these students made of themselves when they tried to scare me with a dead nigger's face when I had slept with a drunken husband for twenty years!'' (121)

Equating the hideous Negro face with an everyday source of domestic irritation brings the story from the archetypal to the mundane, and together with the effortless reestablishment of the framework's temporal distance—''The crowd mizzled; and we, too, I reckon, between that time and the next upheaving of the sun'' (121)—restores order to the narrative.

Many of the mitigating circumstances which limited racial expression in "The Curious Widow" are absent in "Stealing a Baby." While the Negro in this tale is still passive, his form is now complete: in his medical school morgue the persona discovers a dead "infant a few weeks old lying by the side of its dead mother" (154). Although tiny, this figure fully displays the quality of blackness; with a portentous joke its color is related to disorder: "They were both so black in the face that I would have suspected foul play, had it not been accounted for by the fact that they were Negroes" (154). Most important, the disruptive associations of the Negro here are not directed away from the persona. The medical school student takes the baby specifically for his own use, as an object to dissect, and carries it intimately concealed near his body to a meeting with a wealthy girlfriend, where through an accident it is uncovered. Since the Swamp Doctor narrator is relating the account of a personally influential occurrence much nearer to the narrative present, during his "last course of lectures previous to graduation" (151), it must be assumed that the control customarily obtained through the framework by a temporally distanced narrative voice has lessened authority in this tale. Somewhat unstabilized, the narrative in "Stealing a Baby" is more congenial to expressing the unconscious racial associations of its apparently innocent black figure.

The narrative instability is reflected in the unusual disorder which characterizes the persona's consciousness in this tale. Even before encountering the black infant, we find him "becoming suddenly very faint" (153). In this weakened state, he is especially vulnerable to the figure's powerful unconscious influence. When he sees the black corpse he feels an irresistible attraction to it, which is depicted with a lack of inhibition that presages the depth of racial expression in the tale: "I strove to depart, but something formed a bond of association between that dead nigger baby and myself, which held me to my place with my gaze riveted upon it" (154). In the earlier, more controlled narrative, the suggestion of an intimate relationship between persona and black figure triggered a sharp defensive reaction, and the intent to direct the disruptive associations away was immediately reaffirmed. Here, with the persona's vision as deeply influenced by the black object as was the widow's—now *his* "gaze [is] riveted upon it"—some slight attempt to distance the figure occurs. He again moves to conceal it from sight: "I rolled it, tenderly as if alive, into as small a space as possible, and [tied] it up in my handkerchief" (154). But the distancing impulse is tellingly ineffectual, indicating that a spiral of unconscious motivation already has been set in motion. Instead of acting further upon it, the persona undermines the strategy of spacing by compulsively placing the package under his cloak. This reinforcement of the relationship's dangerously intimate direction seems to commit the tale to disorder, for the black figure's presence close to the persona's body heightens his disorientation sharply. It "unnerved me completely," he reveals, "and gave me such a tremor as would have passed for a creditable ague" (154).

Now, as the sketch nears its climax, description increasingly resembles disoriented fantasy. Carrying the black infant, the persona meets his fiancée. The first glimpse of her confirms the direction taken by vision in the tale. Formerly she had seemed beautiful; now an image of diseased sight is projected upon her: her features are "red as an inflamed eye" (155). Disorientation extends to the sense of foundation; the pavement is covered "with a thin coat of ice, making the walking for pedestrians very insecure" (155). Into this unstable setting rush violently conflicting figures. From one side comes "the lady's father accompanied by a man that bore a marvellous resemblance to the city marshal!" (155). From the other with "a growl, a loud yell, bowwow-wow! and with mouth distended like an alligator, . . . a huge bulldog sprang at us" (156). Totally disoriented, the young couple whirl and fall, "cross and pile, our inferior extremities considerably intermingled" (156).

In the midst of the disorder, the black figure appears again. But in this disorganized setting it seems sharply altered from its formerly innocent appearance: "My cloak flew open as I fell, and the force of the fall bursting its envelope, out in all its hideous realities rolled the infernal imp of darkness'' (156). With the ordinarily repressed racial associations now subject to expression, its ''hideous'' overtones now its ''realities,'' the rhetoric describing the black infant fairly reverberates with Satanic imagery. The impression of active influence displayed by the figure stems from its relationship with primordial evil; it bursts into view with ''the force of the fall.'' The influence it exerts is dangerously irrational; it seems ''impish,'' with a dark and ''infernal'' meaning. The sense of disorder conveyed by the Negro appears sufficient to produce an effect upon narrative form. For in concluding the tale the narrator intrudes into the story, but not in the conventionally reassuring manner characteristic of the framework. Instead he seems compelled to enlarge the results of the racial encounter, insisting that his contact with the Negro ruined his chances for a stable life as ''the happy head of a family'' (156), and led to his present disoriented condition, denoted by his ''haggard features and buttonless coat'' (156,158). This tale, extensively depicting the Negro's association with unconscious disorder, ends with an ominous distortion of the defensive forms of narration.

Yet in spite of the far-reaching implications of the outburst in ''Stealing a Baby,'' there are limits to its narrative disruption, a fact which suggests a final component of restraint in the tale. The order inherent in the medical school setting appears to have exerted an inhibiting influence upon the story. The last narrative restraints in Lewis's fiction fall away, however, in a context free of social organization, deep in the swamp.

The meaning of the swamp for Lewis is surely open to conjecture: he was drawn to practice there almost immediately after medical school, and he gave his narrator the title of the Louisiana Swamp Doctor, and the name of Madison Tensas, combining Madison Parish and the Tensas River, which ran through the heart of the bayou country. With its ceaselessly shifting borders of land and water, its confusion of spatial and temporal boundaries, the bayou seems a congenial environment for Lewis's unstable personality. The resemblance is ominous: in reinforcing an existing weakness in distinguishing between primary phenomena, the swamp contributes to a further erosion of the capacity for self-control. It is known that Lewis's recklessness reached fatal proportions in the bayou; his death at twenty-five occurred there when he ignored all reasonable restraints and leapt with his horse into a raging stream. In view of the disruptive role the swamp played in Lewis's life, it seems clear that the place exerted a similarly unsettling influence in his autobiographical writing.

"Seeking a Location" describes the sinister influence of the bayou's disorder upon point of view in Lewis's fiction. Initially in this tale, the swamp seems dangerous. The young persona, on a journey into the bayou to establish his medical practice, sees threat everywhere. On a river steamer, he finds himself "seated over twenty thousand kegs of powder" (179), and recognizes the dimensions of the subterranean danger: it would reduce him to "one of the finest instances on record of molecular disintegration" (179). The road into the bayou too is fraught with warning: it is "over knee-deep in mud and dotted with the bones of deceased oxen" (181). Once inside the bayou, the persona is repeatedly subject to the "considerable force" (182) of the swamp current, "impelled" by it toward submerged trees, to "almost certain death" (182), drawn beneath the surface "head and ears under the muddy waters" (182). But with these helpless immersions, a telling shift occurs in the persona's point of view about the swamp. After being "thoroughly drenched" (182), he begins to have "better luck" (183) in the bayou. A strangely violent baptism seems to have taken place, the extent of which is implied by a complete transformation in appearances: "Laying off my cloth, I donned a suit of 'swamp broadcloth'—yellow linsey—which clove to my proportions as if it were an integral portion of my frame" (183). The persona has abandoned his conventional point of view and assumed that of the swamper in which the imperative primordial forces no longer pose a threat. At the end of this tale the swamp's disordered quality defines the point of view; it has become "integral" to the narrative identity.

It is portentous then, that in Lewis's last story, "A Struggle for

Life,'' the persona has now become the Swamp Doctor, a personality at home in the swamp's disorder. As such he is hardly
distinguished from the somewhat older Swamp Doctor narrator,
who tells us he still enjoys living in the bayou. The narrowed
narrative distance and the disorganizing swamp setting from the
start give an intensely subjective tone to the description. A Negro
appears on the edge of the bayou. He seems the culmination of the
grotesque progression seen in the two previous tales: "He was a
Negro dwarf of the most frightful appearance. His diminutive
body was garnished with legs and arms of enormously dispropor-
tionate length. His face was hideous—a pair of tushes projected
from either side of a double harelip" (245). But there is one further
crucial step; this black figure is alive, and accordingly all the
overtones of racial destruction in the earlier tales take on a grimly
explicit quality. The persona's first impression describes a black
figure in which diabolical malevolence is activated by physical
bestiality: "Taking him altogether, he was the nearest resemblance to the orang-outang mixed with the devil that human eyes
ever dwelt upon" (245).

The entrance into the swamp triggers the subjective spiral latent
in Lewis's fiction. The pair almost immediately become lost. The
bayous are deepening with the spring floods, night is falling, and
the persona's vision becomes characterized by a disturbing unre-
liability: "There, far from human habitation, my only companion
a hideous dwarf, surrounded with water, and the night draperied
darkly around, I lay, the cane leaves for my bed, the saddle for my
pillow, the huge fire lighting up the darkness for a space around,
giving natural objects a strange, distorted appearance" (249). The
deepening subjectivity touches all the persona's perceptions.
Sounds too seem distorted: "The night [is] vocal with discor-
dancy" (249). Normal lines of demarcation in his consciousness
blur; "the light sank mingling with the darkness" (249), and he
hallucinates: "I gazed and started involuntarily. Had I not known
it was an owl surrounded with moss that sat upon a stricken tree, I
would have sworn it was the form of an old man, clad in a sombre
flowing mantle" (249).

In a literal way, the disorder of the controlling point of view is projected upon the black man in this tale. As the persona grows disoriented, with apparent inadvertency he pumps the dwarf full of strong brandy. This has the effect of inducing in the Negro a "wild . . . exhilaration in his manner" (247). Such characteristics are in polar contrast to the normally controlled darky stereotype, a fact marked by the persona upon the dwarf's first drunken action: " 'Give me a dram,' he said very abruptly, not prefacing the request by those deferential words never omitted by the slave when in his proper mind" (250). The rhetoric is significant; seen so totally removed from the customary forms of servility, the Negro seems out of "his proper mind." It takes hardly a step to find insanity in the image of this "freed" black man; the dwarf is soon "aroused to maniacal fury" (251). The mad Negro is an image seldom encountered in antebellum fiction, and with reason, for to the Southern imagination insanity for the black was unrelieved; it connoted totally irrational abandon.

A marked increase in the racial imagery's formidable intensity reveals how radical a step the expression of black insanity is for the Southern writer. Racial hatred, lurking in descriptions of the Negro but rarely voiced, erupts: "To my surprise he retorted, 'D—n you, white man, I will kill you ef you don't give me more brandy' " (250). Most tellingly, the dwarf's eyes, traditionally a barometric symbol of a figure's narrative role, now evidence a deeply unconscious content. They display the light and fire which characterizes the most intuitive expressions of archetypal power: the Negro's "eyes [were] flashing and sparkling with electric light" (250). The persona again marks the subjective status of the black dwarf, defining the meaning of the radiant imagery: "His eyes [were] fixed upon me with a demoniac expression that I shall never forget" (250).

Narrative description at this point is committed to expressing an irrationality so extensive as to begin to defy articulation. Under the burden the form of the Negro's image seems to distort: " 'I will kill you,' he again screamed, his fangs clashing and the foam flying from his mouth, his long arms extended as if to clutch me and the fingers quivering nervously" (250). In the two previous tales, the suggestion of such an unstabilizing influence was sufficient to provoke a counter movement toward order in the narrative. In "The Curious Widow" such an impulse involved the transformation of threat into joke in a manner congenial to the Southwestern humor medium. This controlling impulse occurs here too, but in a weakened form. The persona tries to laugh off the danger: as the dwarf "slowly approached me to carry his threat into execution" (251), the vision "presented something ludicrous, and I laughingly awaited his attack" (251). The reaction is ineffectual; in fact it leads to the final step in the process of disorganization. The approaching violent physical contact between black and white it allows constitutes the ultimate taboo in the Southern imagination; as that inhibition falls, so does the last barrier to unconscious expression. The contact brings a hopeless sense of envelopment: "With a yell like a wild beast's, he precipitated himself upon me. Evading my blow, he clutched with his long fingers at my throat, burying his talons in my flesh and writhing his little body around mine strove to bear me to earth" (251). The embrace is entirely malevolent, the force seems irrationally limitless; engulfed by it the persona experiences a sense of inexorable dissolution: "A mountain, heavier than any earth's bosom holds, was pressing upon my breast, slowly crushing me to fragments" (251).

Descriptive forms seem to have reached their limits in depicting this Southern nightmare. The persona's perceptions become dominated by a curious quality, turning inward. He hears his own pulse: "Its wild singing was in my ears like the ocean wave" (253). Most closely focused on the demonic black figure, the forms of vision waver, dissolve, and are overcome by a shapeless diabolical radiance: "My eyes met his. . . . All kinds of colors first floated before my eyes and then everything wore a settled, intensely fiery red" (251). Finally, overwhelmed by the boundless malevolent force, the persona is destroyed: "I ceased to breathe. I was dead. I had suffered the last pangs of that awful hour" (253); "I lay dead—dead as mortal ever becomes" (254). The narrative continues, with a feeble attempt at justification: "Still in that coffin amidst those writhing worms would have been the immortal mind, and still would it have thought and pondered on till the last day was come. For such is the course of soul and death, as my interpretation has it" (253). But the confusion of the logic suggests the fate of narrative reason in the face of transcendent disorder: this expression of life-in-death displays the evidences of a profound breakdown of rational narrative form. A gauge of just how unhindered by the normal restraints of form the narrative has become at this point occurs in the final, horrified exclamation of the scene. It is in this state that the persona at last makes the identification of the demonic black man's most intimate psychological function. Seeing the drunken black dwarf fallen amidst the raging camp fire, the swamp doctor blurts: "Great God! can that disfigured, half-consumed mass be my evil genius?" (255).

As the tale concludes the persona returns to life. The phenomenon apparently is intended to reestablish credibility for the narrative voice and make possible the invocation of the traditional framework perspective. The narrator steps in to tell us that the dwarf has incinerated himself in his drunken frenzy, and that, led out of the swamp by the mule, he has never "looked again upon the place" (255). But the framework technique primarily draws its authority from a simple assumption of reason in the narrative voice. In this tale the narrator himself has been the victim of the fatal encounter with the black demon. The illogic has introduced a fundamental irrationality into the narrative voice, depriving it of the stable associations necessary for distancing the violence it has related. Facing the obsessive disorder involved in the full expression of the Negro demon, the otherwise effective capacity of the framework to restore order has been undermined. The significance for the Southern writer is unmistakable: even the most apparently stable narrative form in his fiction exists in inverse proportion to the intensity of his expression of the demonic vision.

Chapter Two

Demonic Vision and the Conventions of Antebellum Southern Fiction

In contrast to the situation in Southwestern humor, the extent of racial expression in the antebellum Southern novel seems staggering. The humorists, sketching limited areas of regional color, had the option to select material of a noncontroversial nature. Usually that meant they simply avoided racial expression. But the novelists in one way or another wrote in the service of their society's fundamental dream, the happy plantation. Wistful about the plantation, or critical of its inefficiency, the novelists all were obligated to deal with the bedrock of its economy, the black slave. At the same time, in demonstrating the society's resilience against outside threat, the novelists found a reason for extensive treatment of the Indian. In its commitment to racial expression, the antebellum Southern novel, mostly written during the three decades before the Civil War in the Tidewater South by men such as John Pendleton Kennedy and William Gilmore Simms, offers a vast field for exploring the large-scale effects of demonic vision.

In an era when public statement was subject to powerful censorship, when, as Charles G. Sellers, Jr. puts it, "the South's best minds resolutely quashed their doubts, . . . [and] crisis-tossed editors and politicians took refuge in positive and extreme positions,"[1] the expression of a taboo as basic as racial demonism suffered severe distortion. Primarily of course the depiction of an internal racial threat as extensive as that suspected from the black man was anathema. It was imperative to present the Negro as contented and, above all, harmless. Especially with the approach of the Civil War, Southern novelists acted to purge all traces of danger from their portrayals of the black man. Eventually, through its imbalance, the image of the Negro came to imply its opposite. The caricatures of total black abasement which pervade the Southern novel before the war form, as Guy A. Cardwell points out in the case of the happy plantation house itself, "a working by symbolic substitution, an apotropaic gesture"[2] suggesting the desperate response to an unspeakably profound fear.

The execution of so radical a process of literary repression came at no little cost. Anxieties of the magnitude as those felt about the slave in the antebellum South required an effective outlet. In order to portray the Negro as benevolent, the Southern novelist needed a focus for his racial tensions, a figure receptive to the portrayal of racial hostility, but not subject to social repression. In the antebellum Tidewater South, the Indian was such a figure. By the time the pre-Civil War novels were being written, the red man had long ceased to be a danger to the old coastal society; in fact Indian Removal was completed before most of the works appeared. Since no political or psychological taboo existed upon the expression of savage malevolence, the Indian was the ideal subject for the transferral of tensions stemming from the Negro through the unconscious equation between black man and red. Already serving an explicitly hostile function, the Indian became the recipient of a far greater dimension of racial tension: in the three decades before the Civil War, the Indian served as scapegoat for the Negro in the Southern novelist's imagination.

The influence of this phenomenon upon the antebellum novel was far-reaching. While narratives about the Negro became little more than exercises in wish-fulfillment, the Indian stories assumed a darkly tragic structure by virtue of their immense emotional function. Each work builds to the same racial frenzy: from beginnings characterized by a relatively neutral realism, savage malevolence swiftly dominates the vision of the Indian. Red men become diabolical, either individually, or in a startlingly coalescent form as scattered tribes amass to wage racial warfare upon the whites. Always, cataclysm awaits the Indian. For it is in the inevitable scenes of racial genocide that the Indian novel serves its ultimate role in the antebellum imagination. By focusing his full complement of racial anxieties upon the red man, and then brutally eliminating him, the Southern writer was able to effect at least a momentary catharsis.

Moreover, as these novels move toward their cataclysm, their narratives display the influence of the heightening charge of irrationality conveyed by demonic expression. The voice describing the chaotic frenzy itself becomes disordered, halting, often confused. It seems overcome by fantasy. In this state, sensitized to the unconscious elements of racial vision, the narrative may give voice to the underlying source of the Indian novel's unique subjective intensity. Such moments hold the potential for an explosive depiction of the equation between black man and red.

One further characteristic of the antebellum Southern novel enhanced the possibilities for this psychological process. In its attempt to evade portraying the strained realities of the antebellum South, the Southern novel often moved, as J. V. Ridgely puts it, "not in a world of immediate political upheavals but in one of the imagination."[3] Novelists tended toward the form of the historical romance, which, in William Gilmore Simms's definition, is "imaginative, passionate, metaphysical; [romances] deal chiefly in trying situation [and] bold characterization. . . . They exhibit *invention* in large degree."[4] The freedom inherent in the romance led to "symbolic or allegorical expression. . . . 'Archetypal' situations . . . employed the age-old symbols of light and darkness to typify the . . . struggle between good and evil."[5] In such narrative settings, which tended both to liberate and to heighten subjective symbolism, the manifestations of the diabolical equation flourished.

It is in the fiction of William Gilmore Simms, the foremost practicioner of the historical romance, that the contrasts between black abasement and red devilishness are most dramatic. Simms's treatment of the Negro is the standard for black expression in the antebellum Southern novel. From the period following the end of the racial introspection of the Great Debate in 1831-1832, to the

Civil War, Negro slaves in Southern fiction looked and acted much like those found as early as *The Yemassee* (1835) and as late as *Woodcraft* (1854) and *The Forayers* (1855). These two late works provide good examples of the antebellum novel's treatment of the Negro; Simms conceived of them as answers to Harriet Beecher Stowe's *Uncle Tom's Cabin* (1852) and accordingly placed special emphasis upon the depiction of slavery. Each takes place in a romanticized revolutionary war setting, and in each the devotion of the black slaves to their masters is definitively sentimentalized. In *The Forayers,* for example, one "faithful slave murmured [about his owner], with half a sigh, a tear glistening in his eye as he turned back to his cabin:—'God bress he heart! God bress he heart! I lub 'em like my own chile.' "[6] Interracial physical touching apparently clinches the emotional bond, as in *The Forayers:* " 'You are a cunning rascal, 'Bram' replied the . . . [white owner] with a smile, laying his hand upon the negro's shoulder kindly as he spoke" (18); " 'Good-bye, 'Bram!'—offering his hand. 'God bless you, Mass Willie; God for ebber bless you' " (19). Furthermore, blacks in these works continue a long tradition of endorsing their indentureship, in the case of *Woodcraft* in especially sweeping terms: "Maussa, don't you bodder me wid dis nonsense t'ing 'bout free paper any more. I's well off whar' I is I tell you. . . . I say de wud for all!' "[7]

Emasculated so conclusively in theory, when imagistically conceived the black man appears emasculated in fact. Negroes in antebellum Southern fiction are rarely permitted a sexual virility (Mingo, the amorous Negro in Simms's "Caloya; or, the Loves of the Driver" is one exception, but his exploits are rendered comically, and, in any event, severely punished), and ideally the black man is portrayed as asexual or impotent. One such comfortingly harmless figure appears in *The Forayers* as Ben Bowlegs, whose name itself suggests his fundamental weakness: "Ben Bowlegs, whether because of some natural aversion to the sex, or because of the mature period of sixty-two to which he had arrived, was wifeless and childless. . . . 'Praise de Lawd!' was his occasional exclamation, 'dere's no woman yer to bodder me! Bressings ob de

Lawd, dere's no chillen to dribe de sleep from my eye' " (74).
Another such figure even more fully realizes the ideal of black
emasculation. In *Woodcraft* the personal servant of one Captain
Porgy, the swollen, Falstaffian, former revolutionary war captain
who is Simms's most interesting plantation owner, is symbolically
castrated by his association with traditional women's objects,
kitchen utensils. He is enveloped by them: "The sumpter horse
which he rode was covered . . . with a variety of kitchen equipage.
Pots and kettles were curiously pendant from the saddle, strapped
over the negro's thighs, or hanging from his skirts" (51). He
seems imprisoned by them: "To descend out of his piles, to fling
off . . . pot and kettle, bread and bacon, &c., was, to Tom, a sort
of performance which needed equal discretion and deliberation"
(52). Ultimately, in a moment of racial wish-fulfillment, Simms
envisions the very object of the black man's manhood transformed
into a cooking utensil—and then removed. Later, another character, in helping Tom unload, is seen "almost pulling away the thigh
of the cook in the endeavor to withdraw a gridiron, without first
remarking that it was well strapped to the member" (134).

Such depictions of the Negro, while possibly heightened somewhat in response to late antebellum social conditions, are hardly
different in kind from the image of Hector, the black slave created
by Simms twenty years earlier in *The Yemassee*. Labled "the
adhesive black," Hector is one of the first slaves in antebellum
Southern fiction to defend slavery:

> I dam to hell, mossa, if I guine to be free! . . . 'Tis unpossible,
> mossa, and dere's no use to talk 'bout it. De ting aint right; and enty I
> know wha' kind of ting freedom is wid black man? Ha! you make
> Hector free, he come wuss more nor poor buckrah—he tief out of de
> shop—he get drunk and lie in de ditch—den, if sick come, he roll,
> he toss in de wet grass of de stable. You come in de morning, Hector
> dead—and, who know—he no take physic, he no hab parson—who
> know, I say, mossa, but de debble fine em 'fore anybody else?[8]

Doctors, preachers, care and comfort; Hector's renunciation of
freedom forms an outline in dialect of the standardized Southern

defense of slavery as a benevolent institution.
The Yemassee offers, in fact, a prime example of the expense at
which such contrivance comes. *The Yemassee* is a romance set
during the South's Indian warfare of the early 1700s, and if in it the
Negro is unnaturally benevolent, the Indian can be an inhuman
figure of diabolical proportions. The potential demonic content of
the Indian is signalled early in the novel, in an allegorical episode.
In an idyllic garden, the Southern heroine, standing amongst "the
rich green of the leaves—the deep crimson of the wild flower—the
gemmed and floral-knotted long grass that carpeted the path" (I,
169), encounters an immense serpent, which seems "an evil
presence, . . . [its] star-like eye . . . wooing her to seize" (I,
172-73). The snake in the garden conveys the full measure of
irrational Satanic powers; it effortlessly disorders the girl's consciousness: staring at it

> she felt dizzy, for, as she looked, a cloud of colours, bright, gay,
> various colours, floated and hung like so much drapery around the
> single object that had so secured her attention and spell-bound her
> feet. . . . She strove to move from before the beautiful but terrible
> presence. . . . [But] still the eye glared beautifully bright and pierc-
> ing upon her own. . . . [It] shot forth glances of that fatal power of
> fascination, malignantly bright, . . . paralyzing, with a novel form
> of terror and of beauty. (I, 173-74)

It is soon clear that the serpent is a surrogate for the Indian, that it is
the red man to which the serpent's irrational power refers. As L.
Moffitt Cecil demonstrates, throughout *The Yemassee* "the
coiled rattlesnake, beguiling, malignant, represents the displaced
Indians, now thoroughly aroused and secretly determined to
strike."[9] Accordingly, as the episode ends we find that not only
the rattlesnake in the foliage has observed the maiden, but also
secreted in the garden was a young Indian. And while the red man
slays the serpent, saving the girl, Simms concludes the scene
emphasizing not the differences, but the similarities between
the two devilish figures: "Many of [the Indian's] habits derive
their existence from models furnished by [the rattlesnake's]

peculiarities. . . . It is highly probable, indeed, that, even the war-whoop with which the Indians preface their own onset, has been borrowed from the rattle" (I, 177). The Indian's war-whoop, Simms later insists, arouses "a nameless terror" akin to "such terror as the traveller feels by night, when the shrill rattle of the lurking serpent . . . vibrates all around him" (II, 172).

As the book progresses the Indians increasingly objectify their implicit diabolical content. They become demons in fact to the appalled white protagonists: in "the thick night . . . a thousand enemies, dark, dusky, fierce savages, . . . their wild distortions —their hell-enkindled eyes, . . . the sudden and demoniac shrieks from the women—the occasional burst of song, pledging the singer to the most diabolical achievements, mingled up strangely in a discord" (II, 78). Viewing this image of bedlam in the Southern blackness, it seems that "the demon was aroused, and, once aroused, was sleepless" (II, 78). With all the primordial power initially symbolized by the serpent now focused upon its ultimate object, the red man, the narrative point of view undergoes a striking transformation. A white Cavalier, whose voice dominates the novel, sees the red men not with his usual clearsightedness, but through a vision characterized by "excited thoughts and fancy" (II, 78).

In this subjectively sensitized state, the narrative is primed to express the deep sources of Indian demonism. Peering through a gap in some foliage, the white protagonist recounts a scene which in its broad archetypal frame seems to portend the emergence of a fundamental unconscious content. The Cavalier sees, bound to a tree, arms upward and palms outward, a captive Irishman. While he watches, in a moment of frozen action, "the arrow of one [Indian] penetrated one palm, while that of another, almost at the same instant, was driven deep into the other" (II, 70). The extremes of good and evil can hardly assume a more primary form in the Christian imagination; within the context of this crucifixion nightmare the foundation of the Indian's devilishness is painfully expressed. In staccato, explosive dialogue, the Irishman blurts: "Ay, ye miserable red nagers,—ye don't frighten Tedd Macnamara now so aisily" (II, 68), "ye red divils, . . . ye little red nagers" (II, 69), "you bloody red nagers" (II, 70), "ye red-skinned divils, . . . ye monkeys, and ye alligators, and ye red nagers; and them's the best names for ye, ye ragamuffin divils that ye are" (II, 71). Bestiality, diabolism; in the Irishman's imagistic language, the primordial well-springs of racial demonism indeed seem reflected.

Following the identification, a coalescent red demonism sweeps *The Yemassee*. The amassed tribes attack the coastal colonies in a climax of orgiastic ferocity and are purged from the land. The narrative at last depicts them "broken—without concert—hopeless of all further effort—flying in every direction; shot down as they ran into the open grounds, and crushed" (II, 240). Ultimately, the last of the Indians, the childless old wife of the Yemassee's dead chief, is led away "unconscious of all things . . . save that the Yemassee was no longer the great nation." (II, 242).

Finally catharized, the attitude toward the Indian turns almost nostalgic, the narrative becomes tranquil, its defensive tone relaxed. In the very last lines of the novel there is an apparently unguarded moment. Yet the demonic racial attitudes in the South were pervasive, elusive; purged in one area they merely surfaced in another. With the Indians gone and the narrative unguarded, a jarring image of destructive *Negro* ferocity erupts for an instant, in the barely disguised form of a black army sweeping up after the retreating red men:

> The pursuers were at hand, in the negroes, now scouring the field of battle with their huge clubs and hatchets, knocking upon the head all of the Indians who yet exhibited any signs of life. As wild almost as the savages, they luxuriated in a pursuit to them so very novel—they hurried over the forests with a step as fleet, and a ferocity as dreadful —sparing none, whether they fought or plead, and frequently inflicting the most unnecessary blows, even upon the dying and the dead. (II, 241-42)

The importance of this vision lies not in the direction of the violence but in its form. In their assumption of destructiveness, their luxuriance in it, the Negroes express for an instant the very vision of disorder which to this point had been channeled into the figure of the Indian. In this sense suggesting the failure of the impulse completely to purge racial tension from the narrative, the final flare-up of black ferocity demonstrates the tenacity of racial demonism.

It is this pattern which persists in Indian fiction with minor variations from *The Yemassee* to Simms's *The Cassique of Kiawah* (1859). In this late historical romance Indian diabolism is identified in the vernacular voice by one Jack Belcher who exclaims: "The red devils! call *them* human? I'd as soon trust a monkey, or a sucking tiger, in the matter of human bowels and affection!"[10] As the scattered tribes mass for war on the whites, the red man's demonic associations coalesce, and he once more emerges fully as a figure of supernaturally evil dimensions:

> The appearance of this Iawa [the medicine man] was frightful in the extreme. He was of immense size and stature, nearly seven feet in height, . . . and he wore a head-dress of buffalo-horns in a fillet of feathers. . . . His contortions, savagely frantic and fantastic, as he threw his hands up in air, and whirled through the masses, gashing his breast till the blood issued from every part of it, struck awe and terror even into the souls of those who . . . had long been familiar with such savage rites. . . . [He seemed] a terrible necromancer, calling up the dead and dismal inhabitants of the infernal abodes. (581)

Understandably, however, in view of the portentous publication date, little relaxation of racial defenses accompanies the extermination of the Indian tribes; in *The Cassique of Kiawah* no army of savage Negroes appears to conclude the narrative.

A suggestive variation on this theme occurs in one of Simms's short stories, "The Two Camps," collected in *The Wigwam and the Cabin* (1845). Again employing a historical setting, in this case the border country between North and South Carolina in the early 1700s, as its title implies this tale outlines a split in the imaginative conception of the Indian. On one hand, the narrative deals with a noble young Indian, who had stayed with the white narrator and his wife and daughter for a time, and had returned to persuade the white girl to marry him. This Indian is treated with the romanticism which Albert Keiser shortsightedly sees as characteristic of most of the author's Indian depictions.[11] Simms describes him as "a monstrous fine-looking fellow, tall and handsome, and he was dressed in his very best. He wore pantaloons, like one of us, and his hunting shirt was a raally fine blue, with a white fringe. He wore no paint, and was quite nice and neat with his person."[12] But if the red man's nobility seems to depend upon his particular resemblance to the white frontiersman, there are other Indians in the tale, and *they* appear as black as Negroes: one is "a stout, dark-looking fellow, one-half of whose face was painted black as midnight, with a red circle round both his eyes" (53). Another also wears "the black paint on his face, and the red ring about his eyes" (69). These Indians objectify their blackness; they are totally evil. The two contest for dominance in the narrative, and the malevolent red man eliminates the good Indian in a savage conclusion, "striking—once, twice, three times—hard and heavy, right upon the face and forehead of the young prince" (69). The bloody ending resolves the narrator's dilemma, for the young chief had been proposing marriage to his daughter at the moment of his murder. It also, in the brutality of the good Indian's death, implies the limits upon the Southerner's positive vision of the Indian.

The conclusion of "The Two Camps" is especially telling. The white narrator, who had been spying from a distance upon his daughter and the young Indian, observes the murder. It works a dramatic change in him. He kills the malevolent savage with his rifle, recalling that in a frenzy, "I gave one whoop for all the world as if I was an Indian myself, and run out to the spot" (70). It is as if the sight of the devilish Indian emerging from the woods to murder his daughter's red suitor had given form to a murderous impulse within himself underlying his declared ambivalence over the possibility of miscegenation. In the unusually intimate first-person

narrative of "The Two Camps" there is a shadow of the
psychological basis of racial expression: involuntarily, the white
narrator hints that Indian violence serves as a projection of his own
darker self.

It is such a revelatory function that justifies including in this
discussion a work not strictly Southern in origin, Robert Montgomery Bird's *Nick of the Woods*. While Bird was a Philadel-
phian, and his work appeared there in 1837, his imagination was
drawn to the South, and he traveled extensively in the Southwestern frontier Indian country gathering information for his writing.
Moreover, Bird's novel largely follows the pattern for antebellum
racial fiction. Its plot is comprised of a series of Indian battles
strung upon the journey of a Virginia Cavalier and his aristocratic
lady cousin through Indian territory to make claim to certain
estates. As in the other Indian fiction, while the red man's chaotic
diabolism intensifies, the predominantly white point of view
seems overwhelmed with irrationality: observing devilish red
savagism, the Cavalier "seemed even to himself to be in a dream,
the sport of an incubus, that oppressed every faculty and energy of
spirit, while yet presenting the most dreadful phantasms to his
imagination. . . . The nightmare oppressed mind and body
together."[13] And, as in the other fiction, the intensification of
subjectivity in the point of view liberates the deeply unconscious
source of the demonic attitudes. In this instance the diabolical
equation is expressed in the vernacular voice of a ring-tailed
roarer: "H'yar, you bald-head, smoke-dried, punkin-eating redskins! you half-niggers! you 'coon-whelps! you snakes! . . . I'm
the man to take 'em—cook-a-doodle-doo!" (183); "you exflunc-
tified, perditioned rascal, . . . you niggur-in-law to old Sattan,
you 'tarnal half-imp, you" (277).

Yet Bird pushes beyond this point, to a discussion of the role of
Indian diabolism in the American imagination so intuitive as to
warrant R.W.B. Lewis's suggestion that the work "almost rises,
for an instant or two, to the great fictional stature that the matched
forces [of archetypal good and evil] made possible."[14] With the
crescendo of racial demonism, as the Indian's "shouts became

more frequent and multitudinous, and the village . . . seemed
given up to the wildest and maddest revelry, to the sway of
unchained demons" (337), Bird's narrative suggests that the savage disorder is not inherent to the Indian, but rather projects a
quality deep within the psyche of all men. These visions of the
Indian "enforce the conviction that there is something essentially demoniac in the human character and compostion; as if, indeed, the earth of which man is framed had been gathered only
after it had been trodden by the foot of the Prince of Darkness"
(368).

Before "an army of avenging white-men" (371) arrives to
exterminate the Indians, the narrative objectifies this rare insight,
and in the process resolves the novel's central paradox, concerning
its title character, Nick of the Woods. This shadowy figure is
consistently seen in a contradictory manner. Early in the work the
white settlers describe him: to them "he looks more like a devil nor
a mortal man,—a great tall fellow with horns and a hairy head like
a buffalo-bull, . . . [and] wharby we mean *Old* Nick of the
Woods; for we hold him to be the devil, though a friendly one"
(44). The devil, though friendly. The description encapsulates the
character of Nick, otherwise Nathan Slaughter, a formerly gentle
Quaker, who, after the Indians slaughtered his wife and children,
became obsessed with emulating the red man's savagery, scalping
and mutilating all the warriors he could find. Nathan Slaughter
projects both poles of the white psyche; as well as the ordered
civilizing instinct of the white, he personifies the destructive
forces of savage disorder which lie within the unconscious. Nathan
serves as a measure of the narrative's irrational content. As the
work seems given over to chaos, in the final crescendo of red
savagism, Nathan's image is dominated by his darker psychological role; he *becomes* a savage red figure:

Nathan stripped off his coat of skins. . . . [He] supplied its place by
the loose calico shirt he had selected from among the spoils of the
Indian party, throwing over it, mantle-wise, the broad Indian blanket. His head he bound round with the gawdy shawl which he had
also taken from the brows of a dead foeman; and he hung about his

person various pouches and ornamented belts, provided for the purpose. Then, daubing over his face, arms and breast with streaks of red, black, and green point [sic, ''paint''?] that seemed designed to represent snakes, lizards, and other reptiles; he was, on a sudden, converted into a highly respectable-looking savage, as grim and awe-inspiring as these barbaric ornaments and his attire, added to his lofty stature, could make him. (287)

And after the battle, when the forest's demonic red figures are purged, Nathan too disappears from the narrative, ''going no man knew whither'' (395). No wonder, in this novel abounding with diabolical Indians, the devil of the title refers not to a red man, but to the white, Nathan Slaughter.

As dramatic as the transformation of Nathan Slaughter is, possibly the most telling example of the power of the Indian's irrational associations occurs in the disruption of the detached point of view found in Southwestern humor realism. It is worth a glance at Johnson Jones Hooper's tale, ''The 'Tallapoosy Vollantares' Meet the Enemy,'' in his *Adventures of Captain Simon Suggs* (1845), for in it, unlike the case in the antebellum novel, the Indian is initially depicted with the closest objective detail. Against this cool narrative tone, the emerging unconscious tensions contrast sharply.

The tale begins with a description of a setting in which a group of whites observe a game of ''Indian *ballplay.*'' Play dominates the narrative at this point: we are assured that ''not the slightest danger was anticipated''[15] from savage hostility. Indeed, the depiction of the Indian game focuses upon its apparently civilized basis in formal order. There is a regular ball field, ''a level piece of ground, some two or three hundred yards long, . . . the centre ascertained. Goals are designated at each end'' (106). The equipment is familiar: a ''ball—very like that used in games among the whites'' (106). The prize is sophisticated, ''a huge shot-bag of crimson cloth, covered with beautiful bead-work, and filled with . . . silver money'' (105). In fact, the Indians seem to be far more civilized than savage. No devilish redskins; before the game begins the Indians appear as ''copper-coloured sportsmen'' (105).

The Indians in action, however, are anything but self-restrained, dusky sportsmen:

> No idea of the furious excitement into which the players are worked, can be conceived by one who has never witnessed a scene of the kind. They run over and trample upon each other; knock down their antagonists with their ball-sticks; trip them as they are running at full speed. . . . There are two or three hundred—often five—engaged in the sport at once; all naked except the "flap," and in most instances the affair ends in a terrible *melée.*" (106-7)

Indian ways no longer appear civilized; instead, as they "employ all kinds of force and foul playing to win the game" (106), the red men display a distinct absence of form. The vision of savage disorder stirs a latent component in the white imagination, for the narrative tone grows more subjective, darker, heralding the emergence of repressed diabolical overtones: now "the woods resounded with the fierce yells of the naked savages" (107). And dramatically, once the idea of Indian disorder gains force, the focus of the narrative abruptly turns from the game to the question of a violent confrontation between Indians and whites. The description of savage play is subsumed by the discussion of a rumor "that both parties of Indians were determined to make a sudden attack upon all the white men present, and kill them to a man" (107).

This ambiguous threat provokes a startlingly violent reaction on the part of the whites. Instantly they go on the offensive, stealing the prize money and the Indians' horses, attempting to render them less of a danger, and with money and ponies fleeing across a river. With the encounter a reality, deadly racial associations begin to sweep the narrative. A remnant of the initial sense of play for a moment qualifies the expression of Indian danger. The Indian chief is already "foaming and furious. . . . [But he continues] protesting that the whole affair was a joke on his part" (109). As whites face red men with open hostility across the river, however, the unconscious tension overwhelms the last of the narrative good humor, and the Indian emerges fully as a figure of uncontrolled irrationality: he "danced, shouted, raved, bellowed, and snorted in his boundless rage!" (109). At this point, "boundlessness" takes on a new dimension of meaning. The racial image now expresses the implications of its relationship with total disorder; it presents the threat of unconscious irrationality breaching the boundaries of consciousness. Hence the vision of a lone Indian swimming the boundary imposed by the whites between him and them engenders a response totally out of keeping in this ostensibly humorous tale. Clearly the image evokes the deep old diabolical associations in the white imagination, for at the sight all qualifications upon the expression of hostile racial attitudes dissolve, the Indian is identified as "the d—d old *hostile!*" (110), and eliminated by a brutal murder.

Finally, the awareness of the manner through which the expression of the Indian influences narrative form casts additional light upon a controversy which has concerned one of the South's most unique racial fictions, Edgar Allan Poe's *The Narrative of Arthur Gordon Pym* (1838). The dark nature of the racial fantasy in Poe's tale of a sea voyage southward to an all-black island peopled with completely black men who destroy every white but the narrator is not in doubt. Pym, the first-person narrator, describes the place's inhabitants as "the most wicked, hypocritical, vindictive, bloodthirsty, and altogether fiendish race of men upon the face of the globe."[16] Leslie A. Fiedler finds that "the dark hordes of Too-Wit project the image of what the Southerner privately fears the Negro may be,"[17] and Sidney Kaplan sees Poe's black men as "the people of the Prince of Darkness" and the story "an allegorical and didactic damning of the Negro."[18] But the artistic competence of Poe's only long work of fiction is open to question. According to J. V. Ridgely and Iola S. Haverstick, Poe rushed his manuscript, under publisher's pressures, and *Pym* broke up into five separate and sometimes contradictory sections.[19] Robert L. Carringer convincingly argues that this one attempt of Poe's to write novel-length fiction suffers from the author's psychological incompatibility with the narrative form.[20] As Ridgely and Haverstick put it, it seems that "the story lacks a controlling theme, and has no uncontrovertible serious meaning. . . . No amount of straining can bring all its disparate elements into a consistent interpretation.''[21]

Such criticisms apparently account for what seems an inconsistency in the novel's characterization. The southward journey begins with a mutiny led by a black cook and a half-breed Indian. The Negro is seen as "in all respects . . . a perfect demon" (42), and the Indian

> was one of the most purely ferocious looking men I ever beheld. He was short in stature—not more than four feet eight inches high—but his limbs were of the most Herculean mold. His hands, especially, were so enormously thick and broad as hardly to retain a human shape. . . . His head was equally deformed, being of immense size, with an indentation on the crown (like that on the head of most Negroes). . . . The mouth extended nearly from ear to ear, the lips were thin, . . . [and the] ruling expression may be conceived when it is considered that the teeth were exceedingly long and protruding, and never even partially covered, in any instance, by the lips. [He seemed] convulsed with laughter, . . . [but] the merriment must be that of a demon. . . . [There was] a doubt of his sanity. (43)

The Negro is soon killed off, but Peters, the Indian, becomes Pym's companion through the rest of the adventures. However, as Ridgely and Haverstick point out: "There is a marked discrepancy between the character of Peters as he is introduced . . . and as he later appears. . . . The Peters of the drifting sequence [later in the novel] and the Tsalal episode [on the all-black island] has become a different man." Peters's "ferocious appearance and his 'hybrid' makeup are never again alluded to."[22] Ultimately, the Indian seems to have become a white man; Ridgely and Haverstick note that after the island's black natives destroy the ship's crew, Pym refers to Peters and himself as "the only living white men upon the island" (169).

Yet it is in the area of racial characterization that a continuity most discernibly exists in *Pym*. Joseph J. Moldenhauer demonstrates the presence of an unconscious form of progression in the novel, arguing that "the narrative's true substance is its hero: all experience is projected by him before it is actually lived; all exterior places realize the topography of his dreams; all other characters, however friendly or hostile, are his doubles, extensions, personae."[23] In this subterranean manner, the hordes of devilish blacks on Tsalal realize the demonism of the single Negro who initiates Pym on his southward journey. Similarly the Indian's demonism, in this novel not carrying the additional charge of repressed black tensions, develops in a subtler, but still profoundly influential form.

The Indian's lurking irrational overtones become manifest late in the novel. In attempting to escape from the devilish island, Pym and Peters are forced to descend a sheer cliff. Peters does so, but Pym in the process experiences a disruption of point of view similar to that seen in the case of other white protagonists in desperate racial situations; he feels his "fancies creating their own realities, and all imagined horrors crowding upon me" (185). Pym surrenders his point of view to fantasy: "With a wild, indefinable emotion half of horror, half of a relieved oppression, I threw my vision far down into the abyss" (185). Looking symbolically into the depths of the unconscious, the narrative expresses a vision which accounts for the early devilishness of the Indian's description, and makes clear that in spite of the apparent lapse in characterization the demonism fundamental to the conception of the red man has undergone a process of development. Through this point of view, with "a spinning of the brain," Pym sees Peters as "a dusky, fiendish, and filmy figure [who] stood immediately beneath me" (185). In his hazy dark fiendishness, the Indian seems now to express an irrational power far more deeply subjective than that suggested simply by his initially grotesque appearance. In fact, while after this incident the Indian resumes his overtly benevolent role, there is no longer a doubt of his surreal associations. Escaping the island, Pym, a captive all-black native, and Peters drift toward the South Pole, which in this fantasy is a place of warmth and milkiness. Both dark figures seem to evidence an intuitive understanding of the Pole's fundamental unreason.

The Negro is driven by it to convulsions and death, while the Indian presents an inscrutable look, "an expression I could not fathom" (193); from Pym's point of view an inexplicable embrace of the impending irrationality. Such a dark alliance with unreason is fundamental to the demonic racial vision. It accounts for the earlier doubts about Peters's rationality, about his sanity. The final expression of the red figure's irrational content subtly realizes the implications of the initial demonic portrayal and forms yet another covert strand comprising the novel's underlying narrative continuity.

The demonism of Poe's portrayal of the Indian is in keeping with antebellum practice, but his abandoned treatment of the Negro in *Pym* is of course atypical of the pre-Civil War Southern novel. *Pym* is hardly comparable to the plantation novel format at all. In a sense the radical departure in form and content in the work stems from the ambivalence in Poe's own social position: he shared the paradox in regard to his Southern allegiances that accounted for the freedom in racial treatment seen in the work of Henry Clay Lewis. But for a brief period in the pre-Civil War South it was possible for the conventional Southern author, writing in the established plantation novel form, to portray the black man, if not with the ferocity seen in *Pym*, at least with a certain latitude of expression. During the moment of racial introspection which accompanied the Great Debate over slavery in 1831-1832, the forms of repression directed at the depiction of the Negro which were to so severely influence the antebellum Southern novel had not yet assumed their full rigidity. Consequently, the image of the Indian had not yet swelled in importance. In the few novels produced during this period the black man is the focal point of racial expression, and within narrow limits his portrayal is at least free to hint at the existence of the massive undercurrents of racial demonism in the Southern mind.

John Pendleton Kennedy's *Swallow Barn* (1832) is the work which dominates the earliest antebellum fiction. Kennedy was the prototype of the introspective early antebellum Southern novelist. His detachment from the most conservative Southern institutions was marked. Most of his life was spent in the upper South, in Baltimore, he was married into a successful merchant family; as William R. Taylor points out, "Kennedy never, even momentarily, deviated from sentiments which were from the beginning Unionist and nationalist."[24] At the same time, however, Kennedy was subject to the powerful lure of the Southern myth: "In his speeches and addresses he talked of Saxon ancestry, discoursed on the manners of the Old Dominion and reminisced about Cavalier Maryland."[25] In the early 1830s, as Ridgely puts it, Kennedy's attitudes about the South displayed "the tension . . . of a man who could be drawn both to the Southern past and the national future."[26]

Accordingly, in the general format of his fiction, Kennedy treated Southern institutions with an uneasy irony, an ambivalence which manifests itself in the narrative as a certain instability. As Ridgely suggests, the narrator of *Swallow Barn*, Mark Littleton, a Northerner visiting the plantation of Virginia relatives, "is *both* outsider and insider; he is a Northerner but also kinsman to a large, closely knit Southern clan. His independence weakens and his critical eye wavers; he finds himself extolling the life of the region as well as occasionally unmasking its faults and foibles."[27] In regard to the Negro, however, Kennedy's irony is less apparent. Jean Fagan Yellin points out that "despite the satirical tone Kennedy uses in describing much of Virginia life, he does not handle the Southern 'peculiar institution' ironically."[28] In the sensitive area of racial description, the narrative point of view often seems stabilized in the dark mode of "a Northerner whose prejudices have been shaken by direct observation."[29]

Just how tentative Kennedy's capacity for unrepressed racial portrayal is can be seen in two of his novels produced after the period of racial introspection had passed. Works such as *Horse Shoe Robinson* (1835) and *Rob of the Bowl* (1838) form a pair, with the earlier novel falling into the pattern of stereotyped black racial expression, and the later, standardized romance of Indian warfare serving as the subject for the tranferral of repressed tensions about the Negro. Dialogue—" 'Haw, haw, haw!'—

chuckled Tony; 'Think I don't know how to take care of a hos, mass! . . . Bless the gentman!' ''—and philosophy—benevolence is ''that facility which distinguishes [the Negro] race,—the most uncaring and happiest of mortals''[30]—in *Horse Shoe Robinson* is hardly distinguishable from the usual antebellum description of the black man, while the pattern of demonic crescendo and purgation in the portrayal of the red man in *Rob of the Bowl* fulfills the cathartic function required of the pre-Civil War Indian novel.

It is predictable then that in *Swallow Barn* descriptions of the Negro normally take the form of the conventional Sambo stereotype. There is Scipio, a black servant as usual devoted to maintaining the social system by which he is indentured: ''Scipio, though black, had all the unction of an old gentleman. He had a great deal to say of the 'palmy days' of Virginia, and the generations which in his time . . . had gone 'over the mountain.' He expatiated, with a wonderful relish, upon the splendors of the old fashioned style in that part of the country; and told me very pathetically, how the estates were cut up, and what old people had died of, [sic, ''off''?] and how much he felt himself alone in the present times . . . importing an affectionate attachment to the old school, of which he considered himself no unworthy survivor.''[31] And there is ''a pragmatical old negro, named Carey, who, in his reverence for the occupation, is the perfect shadow of his master, . . . 'a faithful old cur' '' (I, 31-32). Theoretical passages, following established patterns, support the stereotype: the children have ''a predominant love of sunshine, . . . lazy, listless postures, and apparent content to be silently looking abroad'' (II, 225). Blacks in general are ''a comparatively comfortable and contented race of people, with much less of the care and vexation of life than I have often observed in other classes of society'' (II, 227). Most ''desired no greater liberty than [they] then enjoyed, and would not entertain the idea of any possible separation from the [white] family'' (II, 238).

In spite of such stereotyping, scattered throughout the book in environments that act to erode consciousness, at night by firelight, for example, the image of the Negro moves closer to betraying its subjective source. One such instance demonstrates the fundamental dependence of demonic expression in this work upon a liberating situation. Framed by two digressions involving the supernatural, a journey into "the Goblin Swamp," a place of "long and distorted shadows" (I, 297) containing the ruins of the home of one Mike Brown, "who had strange doings with the devil" (I, 298), and Mike Brown's tale itself, the "Chronicle of the Last of the Virginia Devils," the narrator chances in the darkness to see a nearby group of Negroes. Influenced by the context of heightened subjectivity, and spurred by the diabolical references, Littleton views the black people in a rare new light: "There were sundry wide-mouthed negroes, children and grown, who were clustered into a dusky group beneath the parlour window, just where a broad ray of candlelight fell upon them; and who displayed their white teeth, like some of Old Nick's own brood, as they broke out now and then into hysterical, cowardly laughs" (II, 3). This image still shows traces of repression; if the Negroes cannot be harmlessly good-natured, at least they safely can be "cowardly." But they do appear "like some of Old Nick's brood," and most important, their laughter hints at an ominous hysteria, an implicit content of disorder.

Elsewhere in *Swallow Barn,* racial expression may take a similarly suggestive form. In one instance, during an account of a sleepy summer morning on the plantation, a second and even more ominous note intrudes into the description of the Negro. Encountering the "numerous herd of little negroes about the estate," the plantation owner and the narrator set about to find "a new diversion" (II, 57). The episode depicts a comical footrace among the black children, and also a mockery of black militantism, in which "these young serfs [have been] drilled . . . into a kind of local militia. . . . They have an old watering-pot for a drum, and a dingy pocket handkerchief for a standard, under which they are arrayed in military order. As they have no hats amongst them . . . each stick[s] a cock's feather in his wool; and in this guise they parade over the grounds with a riotous clamour" (II, 59). Yet behind the disarming mask of humor the vague notion of an organized black army apparently touches a raw nerve in the Southern imagination, for sandwiched between the two descriptions the narrator again experiences the vision of a repressed unconscious power in the image of the Negro. For a moment, on spying "their white teeth in striking contrast with their complexions" (II, 58), Littleton blurts out an image of supernatural racial associations: "They are a strange pack of antic and careless animals, and furnish the liveliest picture that is to be found in nature, of that race of swart fairies which, in the old time, were supposed to play their pranks in the forest at moonlight" (II, 58).

Such moments form a *leitmotif* in *Swallow Barn*, expressing a subterranean racial ambivalence which finally surfaces in a manner that confirms its centrality and implies the extent of its influence in the Southern imagination. For *Swallow Barn* ends with a treatment of the explosive idea of Negro rebelliousness. This material is described in a tale within the fictional narrative, an expressive technique which offers the safeguard of additional narrative distance, since of course the tale describes events occuring at some time in the past and often in a remote place. The story presents an implacably defiant slave, Abe, "the most irreclaimable of culprits. He molested the peace of the neighbourhood by continual broils; [and] was frequently detected in acts of depredation upon the adjoining farms" (II, 240). He "had once brought himself into extreme jeopardy by joining a band of out-lying negroes, who had secured themselves, for some weeks, in the fastnesses of the low-country swamps, from whence they annoyed the vicinity by nocturnal incursions of the most lawless character" (II, 240-41). And Kennedy, apparently secure within the highly controlled narrative detachment, treats the emotionally charged black figure with the rarest objectivity. He accounts for the black's rebelliousness as stemming from positive qualities such as "spirit, . . . passion, . . . coupled with singular shrewdness of intellect" (II, 239). "Courage" and fearlessness lead to his dissatisfaction with servitude.

But this racial portrait involves a variation of the paradox which

Taylor identifies as resulting from Kennedy's ambivalence, "a form of emotional Indian giving."[32] Kennedy's objectivity becomes in fact a form of self-deception, a mask behind which the narrative moves inexorably to purge the danger unreasonably linked with the Negro. Evidences of an irrational content in this episode occur early. In envisioning Abe's noble character, Kennedy merely inverts the standard racial cliches: the Negro shows "nothing of the flat nose and broad lip of his tribe," and displays "a frame . . . well knit, and of uncommonly symmetrical proportions for the race to which he belonged" (II, 239). Moreover, as Yellin points out, Abe's fearless features would have been reminiscent of the dangerous black men of the West Indies,[33] notorious for their massacres at Santa Domingo. Kennedy's unconscious associations with black defiance, however, are still deeper. After the slave's attempt at escape, his owner consigns him as an indentured sailor on the Chesapeake Bay. Abe thrives, becomes an exemplary seaman, and in his bravery volunteers to face a terrific storm to save a foundering boat. Professing admiration for the gesture, Kennedy nevertheless is compelled also to express a darker interpretation of it. A white seaman voices the deeply irrational attitude toward black defiance: "Well, . . . a negro that is born to be hanged—you know the rest, Abe:—the Devil may help you, as he sometimes does" (II, 254).

Demonism and death: the sailor's warning carries the two poles that recur in Southern racial fiction wherever the dark figure is given sufficient latitude of expression. In the case of the Negro, as well as with the Indian, as the threatening diabolical content moves toward dominance, the counter impulse to eliminate the dangerous figure, to restore order to the narrative becomes apparent. The tendency toward repression in regard to the dark figure has many variations; it may seem that Abe's fate to be lost in the storm, his death never fully ascertained, is far less decisive than the wholesale genocide observed in the Indian fiction. Yet the death of this Negro plays an unsuspectedly fundamental role in *Swallow Barn*. It is not merely that Abe is the only character in this generally light-hearted novel to meet such a grim fate; rather it is most striking that the book ends with the Negro's disappearance. The first words from the narrator to follow Abe's tale are: "The time had now arrived when it was necessary for me to return to New York" (II, 268). In spite of its narrative remoteness, the unresolved story of black rebelliousness brings this otherwise rambling novel to an end.[34] It is as if Kennedy, coming suddenly to face the extent of his own racial irrationalities, had been compelled to break off his treatment of Southern ways, forced to retreat from the unusually candid description of contemporary Virginia in order to escape the tragic basis of his, and ultimately the Southerner's, cultural ambivalence.

Chapter Three

"A Plan to Wake the Devil": Race and Aesthetics in the Tales of George Washington Harris

Sut Lovingood, the narrator-protagonist of George Washington Harris's *Sut Lovingood Yarns* (1867), rightly has been called "the uncrowned king of pranksters in native American humor."[1] In these tales of half-frontier life in the mountain country of Tennessee and North Carolina, written mostly before the Civil War, Sut's practical jokes constitute more than half of the plots.[2] In each of those stories Sut, disrupting social gatherings and furiously attacking figures of authority, displays the essence of the trickster, as Karl Kerényi defines him, appearing "the spirit of disorder, the enemy of boundaries."[3] At such times there is a sense of inexorableness to Sut's actions; Paul Radin suggests the trickster is "constrained to behave as he does from impulses over which he has no control."[4] During quieter moments Sut comments upon this facet of his personality, labling himself "a natural-born durned fool,"[5] and complaining "I thinks at random, just as I talk and does. I can't help it. I'se got no steering oar to my brains" (200). "Confusion," as Lewis Leary insists, "is part of [Sut's] character, even of his intention, and should not be tampered with."[6] For in his most important role Sut is the unconsciously motivated trickster: himself disordered, he invokes further disorder with an almost total abandon. As trickster, his function, as Radin describes it, in "the tales told about him, is to add disorder to order and so make a whole, to render possible, within the fixed bounds of what is permitted, an experience of what is not permitted."[7]

Such qualities are not, however, those which account for the impressive acclaim accorded Harris from critics and writers alike. Southern authors, including Mark Twain and William Faulkner, have known, admired, and sometimes drawn upon the *Yarns*.[8] Critics such as F. O. Matthiessen have suggested that "Harris possesses on the comic level something of what Melville does on the tragic."[9] Kenneth S. Lynn calls Harris "the most gifted humorist to come out of the Southwest before Mark Twain."[10] Eugene Current-Garcia maintains that "the imaginative world . . . [Harris] created, . . . chiefly through the voice of his central character, Sut Lovingood, remains unsurpassed in nineteenth-century American fiction."[11] Common to all the praise is the sense of Harris's impressive aesthetic capacity. If his narrator-protagonist embodies the spirit of disorder, Harris in his public life was "dignified, formal,"[12] and in his writing was equivalently concerned with the problems of style. Echoing Walter Blair, Milton Rickels points out that "the skill and intelligence of [his] revisions permits the generalization that Harris was the most self-conscious and the most resourceful craftsman of all the humorists of the Old Southwest."[13] Especially through the subtle "counterpoint of the imagery" Harris reveals his serious intent, "sounding the deeper discords of the American Eden."[14] Surely with the exception of Edgar Allan Poe and possibly William Gilmore Simms, Harris has fair claim to being the antebellum South's most accomplished artist.

The two poles of Harris's artistic personality, special concern with aesthetic form coupled with quintessentially disordered content, brought about a highly complex situation in regard to racial expression. Harris's impulse toward disorder led inevitably to an involvement with figures of blackness. Sut, setting out to evoke chaos in the tales, sometimes makes use of animals with traditionally violent attributes—wild bulls or horses, for example—but in those tales which move furthest toward the depiction of irrationality this uniquely Southern prankster is drawn to tap the deep font of disordered racial associations in the Southern imagination.[15] The process occurs in a way which reflects the sophistication of Harris's aesthetic capacity. Sut does not simply encounter gro-

tesque Negroes, as does Henry Clay Lewis's narrator; he creates
them with paints and brushes, using the tools of the artist in a
macabre metaphor of the process of demonic expression in Southern fiction. It is a grim inversion of the intent of the minstrel show.
Practicing with his black paint upon the faces of living bodies (and
sometimes dead ones) of indiscriminate color, Sut produces not
the coveted image of total black benevolence but the feared one of
transcendent black diabolism. Similarly, Harris's stylistic
accomplishment lends special definition to the repressive counter
impulse incurred by the disorder. In a sense Harris shares his
fellow humorists' reluctance about depicting the Negro. For in his
creation of these black figures he is neither treating the black man
realistically nor stereotypically. Rather, in a manner anticipating
the fiction of Mark Twain and William Faulkner, Harris presents
the first exploration of the metaphoric uses of blackness in Southern fiction.

One of the tales in which Sut plays prankster, "Old Skissim's
Middle Boy," dramatically illustrates the process. The story
begins as usual for Harris's writings: a minor character irritates
Sut, and upon this hapless person Sut focuses the full force of his
disordering impulse. It is understandable in this case, for the
subject is "a dreadful fat, mean, lazy boy" who "could beat a hog
and a hungry dog eatin" (17). But what arouses Sut most about the
boy is his continual sleeping: "They waked him to eat, and then
had to wake him agin to make him quit eatin; waked him to go to
the spring, and waked him to start back agin; waked him to say his
prayers, and waked him to stop sayin them. In fact, they were
allers a-wakin him, and he were allers a-goin to sleep agin"
(17-18). No wonder this sleeping figure obsesses Sut, leading him
to "lay wake of nights for a week, fixin the way to" (18) make the
boy the subject of his prank. He is the perfect subject for the
trickster. In his formless sleep Sut sees a virtually limitless piece of
unconsciousness upon which to work. The boy is a figure with an
irresistible potential for irrationality.

Sut identifies his prank in a manner which anticipates a full
realization of the sleeper's potential for disorder. Coming upon the

boy alone in his family's kitchen "sittin onto a split-bottom chair, plumb asleep all over, even to his ole hat" (19), Sut indicates that the trick he is about to play is indeed one to evoke primordial chaos; that it is "a plan what I thought would wake the Devil" (19). Carrying it out, Sut employs his brush and black paint to transform the sleeping boy into a figure not yet a devil, but a step closer to it in the Southern imagination because of the associations of blackness: "I had him safe now to practice on, and I set in to doin it, sorta this way. I painted his face the color of a nigger coal-burner, except a white ring round his eyes. From the corners of his mouth, sorta downwards, slouch-wise, I left a white strip. It made his mouth look sorta like onto a hoss track and nigh onto as big" (20). At this point the figure is hardly distinguishable from a minstrel darky, yet Sut is out for chaos, and the direction the creation will take is implicit in his point of view. He sees it as "a fine picture to study if your mind were fond of scary things" (20); it gives him "dreams of the Devil" (20).

Accordingly, Sut goes on to fill in on this black canvas the forms inherent to the Southerner's "picture" "of the Devil." As has been discussed, fundamentally they involve fire. Sut gives his creation the potential for hell-fire, tying "a basket full of fire-crackers to the chair back, to his hair, and to his wrists" (20). Furthermore, he magnifies the figure's capacity to objectify the destruction integral to the demonic vision; Sut "screwed onto each of that boy's ears a pair of iron hand-vices. . . . They hung down like over-growed earrings. I tied a gridiron to one ankle and a pair of firetongs to t'other" (20). There is no mistaking the malevolence underlying the image now: Sut has created a vision of the Southern racial nightmare, and its destructive energies tremble on the verge of eruption: "He looked savage as a set steel trap baited with arsenic, and were just fit for treason, stratagem, and to spoil things" (20).

Even so, the evidence of the depth of this figure's unconscious associations is stunning. When Sut activates his black-faced devil, turning "loose a pint of June bugs . . . into his bosom and . . . a big, grey-whiskered, aggravated ole rat . . . into the slack of that boy's britches'' (20), the force that flows into it seems overwhelmingly primordial: he began to wake ''sorta gradually—a little faster nor light bread rises and a little slower than a earthquake wakes weasels'' (21). The image is surely a likely one, for combining the inexorable quality of bread rising with the sense of the earthquake's limitless subterranean power, the figure seems destined irresistibly to grow to transcendent proportions. With his firecrackers lighted, he does become a fiery black being of supernatural energies: ''He fought by the light of ten million sparks; he were as active as a smut-machine in full blast and every grain of wheat a spark,'' crying ''Gloree,'' causing an ''unearthly riot'' (22).

Expressing what has now become a content of primal disorder places inordinate strain on Harris's formidable capacity for aesthetic form. To depict it he is driven to the sort of surreal imagery we have come to associate with movie cartoon violence: arms extending and multiplying with greater and greater rapidity, the frenzied figure ''grabbed the fire shovel and bounced . . . all over that kitchen, a-striken over-handed, under-handed, up-handed, down-handed, and left-handed at every 'spicious shadow he seed'' (22). Still the content of disorder grows: ''He made more fuss, hit more licks at more things, were in more places and in more shapes in a shorter time than any mortal auctioneer could tell if he had as many tongues as a basket full of buckles'' (22). Beyond even the capacity of an auctioneer to articulate: the figure's level of irrationality must indeed be high. But the homely vernacular language should not distract from the sophisticated concept Harris delineates By indicating that a virtual infinity of expressive organs is still inadequate to portray the ''shapes,'' to pin down the ''places'' of the activity, Harris is in effect acknowledging that the demonic black figure has passed beyond the author's limits of aesthetic form. Carrying his expression of the demonic vision to its ultimate extreme, Harris is faced with the dilemma of having evoked an imaginative quality which now seems to defy the control implicit in the process of aesthetic form.

A sense of helplessness now sweeps the narrative. Continuing to grow, the violence becomes seen as "unquenchable" (25), in its infinity of energy seeming "perpetual-motion" (24). Harris finally employs the framework technique by means of concluding the tale and reestablishing narrative perspective, a ploy which Walter Blair has suggested is essential for the continuation of the *Yarns's* humorous intent.[16] Yet even within this stylistic security, there is a grimness which is absent from Harris's nonracial fiction. The disruption in the tale has extended beyond the kitchen; old man Skissim has been frightened off, and the rest of the family wounded in various ways. Even a final attempt at distance, Sut's resumé of the action, speaks of mass murders and of Sut's jarringly malign impulse to eliminate the figure with "a musket and sixteen buckshot at just about ten steps" (25). The boy's frenzy finally subsides on its own, but instead of a catharized tranquility, the tale ends with a continuing tension which reflects the unresolved narrative issues.

Sut's evocation of black demonism occurs on a markedly broader scale in another prankster story, "Frustrating a Funeral." Again Sut employs passive figures upon which to create images of the devil, in this case a drunkard and a corpse. The initial step in the process is unnecessary here; both of the subjects are Negroes. The creation follows the now recognizable pattern: upon the stupored black Sut "set in and painted red and white stripes, time about, runnin out from under his eyes like onto the spokes of a wheel . . . and cross-barred his upper lip with white, until it looked like boars' tushes; and I fastened a couple of yearling's horns onto his head, and plaited a dead blacksnake round the roots of 'em" (202-3). Turning to the Negro corpse, Sut

> got 'bout a tin cupful of lightnin bugs and cut off the lantern of the last durned one. I smeared 'em all over his face, hair, and ears, and onto the prongs of a pitchfork. I set him up in the corner on end and give him the fork, prong-end up, in his crossed arms. I then pried open his mouth and let his teeth shut onto the back of a live bullfrog; and I smeared its paws and belly with some of my bug-mixture; and pinned a little, live garter-snake by its middle crosswise in Ceaze's mouth, smeared like the frog plumb to the point of his tail. The pin

kept the snake pow'ful busy makin circles and other crooked shapes
in the air. (203)

In one sweep, Sut has created two vividly diabolical black images,
both sharing the basic relationship with hell-fire. The one is "the
awful corpse with its face and hair all afire" (206); the other
displays "eyes and their stripes like buggy wheels with red lamps
in the hubs" (215).

Sut uses each of these figures in the manner of the trickster, to
introduce disorder into the community. The tale is made up of a
series of episodes in which the trickster exposes a number of
pivotal figures in the town to the devilish blacks, reducing each of
them to hysteria. In each episode Sut takes part in the prank,
imitating the devil's voice, using his knowledge of town scandal to
focus the terror being dealt out. With a preacher, Sut "moaned out
in a awful doleful voice: 'Hypocrite, come to hell' " (204). With
an adulterer, "in the same doleful sounds . . . [he] said: 'Hunicutt,
you'se fell from grace. I'll take you down home *now*, lest you
might git good *and die afore you fell agin' " (205)*. With a
grave-robbing doctor he calls: "You wants some bones to boil,
does you? . . . I'se in that business myself—follered it nigh onto
thirty thousand years. . . . Let's go. My boilin house is warm
. . . you'se cold . . . come, sonny" (207). He plays on the guilt
of the sheriff, who had just hanged a Negro: "Rise, Sheriff. He's
a-reachin for you with his rope, *and its got a running noose"*
(215). At one point involving the devilish black corpse, Sut lends
motion to the image, pulling at one victim, pretending to be the
devil, dynamically displaying his disordering impulse: "Right
then and there, I reached out and grabbed his shirt—a saving hold
with both hands—set my cold, sandy foot agin his bare back and
leaned into pullin pow'ful strong" (205).

The technique achieves its goal; the phenomenon of the black
demon loose in white society induces an almost total destruction,
objectifying the Southerner's racial fantasies of social upheaval:
"Hunicutt gone; . . . *doctor* gone; *parson* gone; *sheriff* gone;
and, to cap the stack of vexatious things, the *doggery keeper* gone.

Why, the county's ruinated, . . . you kin buy land there for a dime a acre, on tick at that'' (216). And beyond such concrete disruption there is the shadow of the depth of the forces which have been released by invoking the black demon. Sut indicates that the destruction has a profound subjective racial source; that it is ''the awful consequences of bein scary when a nigger dies'' (216). Touched by the surreal associations of the dark figure, the land is ''haunted yet with all sorts of awful haunts'' (216). Surely the trickster has been drawn to the most effective means of introducing disorder into Southern society.

Yet irrationality in this tale never goes beyond the hint of the surreal. There is of course an eerie quality to the image's movement: ''There were a 'luminated snake a-wavin round; there were the shiny frog movin his legs and paws like he were a-swimmin, . . . there were the [waving] pitchfork with its hot prongs'' (206). At no point, however, does the black demon's motion approach the limits of form as in ''Old Skissim's Middle Boy.'' It is as if in this tale, unlike the other, there is a pervasive narrative guardedness, an inhibiting reluctance to give full reign to the possibilities for disorder inherent in the demonic expression. This is reflected in the unusual presence of a shadowy self-controlled gentleman narrator, a figure whom, as Lynn points out, reveals the ''vestiges of the traditional forms''[17] of controlling narrative techniques in Southwestern humor. Occasionally in the other tales this sophisticated character introduces Sut's account, and retreats, to reappear in the concluding framework. In this story he becomes a sort of interlocutor, continually feeding questions to Sut in remote, jarringly conventional language such as: ''What in the name of the Prophet is 'mill-sick,' Sut?'' (207). Elsewhere, Sut displays exasperation with this repressive figure, crying ''now durn your littil santerfied face'' (Inge, 101). In this instance his stilted, self-conscious interruptions form a counterpoint to Sut's diabolical fantasy, fragmenting it, inhibiting its scope.

At the same time the tendency toward restraint in this sketch takes another, significantly new, shape. While Sut is creating one of the figures, he steps back to admire his work, and puts it in a unique perspective: "And durn my legs if I didn't come nigh onto takin a runnin scare myself, for he were a perfect daguerreotype of the Devil, took while he were smokin mad" (203). The image emphasizes distance, for it removes the demon one step from the foreground, viewing it as a picture within the narrative. But more important, it makes use of the qualities of the photograph which stand in direct opposition to the frenzied irrational associations of demonic vision. The theoretical accuracy of this relatively new scientific instrument to record data leads it to serve as a metaphor for form rendered with definitive control. Sut's daguerreotype fixes the disordered black devil in a totally abstract temporal and spatial form, momentarily capturing it in the conclusive stasis of the photographic image. Occurring again and again in subsequent racial fiction, the photograph objectifies the repressive impulse to control demonic expression.

Harris displays the racial variation on Sut's trickster theme in still another of the *Yarns*. In "Sut Lovingood's Dog," Sut ignites two pounds of gunpowder in a character's pocket, and the prank transforms the unfortunate figure into one whose "face wur as black as a pot, sept a white ring roun his eyes, an' the smoke wur still risin frum amung the stumps ove his burnt har. His hed . . . wus the ugliest, scuriest, an' savidgest site I ever seed or spec tu see in *this* wurld, eny how" (Inge, 126). Once black, Sut labels the figure a murderer: "He's kill'd an 'oman an' nine children, an' I speck a dog, an' like tu whipped anuther plum tu *deth*" (Inge, 126-27). Here the black devil is countered by a less sophisticated strategy: he is simply driven away, leaving a trail which "in sum places the fences wer sot afire" (Inge, 127). But even in this relatively limited instance Harris's vivid aesthetic capacity gives succinct form to the two poles which are inherent to the expression of demonic vision in Southern fiction.

Chapter Four

Tom Sawyer:
The Making of a Safe World

As fundamentally as *Huckleberry Finn* and *Pudd'nhead Wilson*
—which also deal with what Henry Nash Smith calls "The Matter
of Hannibal"—Mark Twain's *The Adventures of Tom Sawyer*
(1876) is a Southern book. There is little question that the South
was a primary influence upon its author. As Kenneth S. Lynn
suggests, "Mark Twain was first and always a Southerner; Southern traits were as fundamental to his personality as Whitman had
noted they were to Lincoln's"[1] A childhood spent in the slave-
holding territory around Florida and Hannibal, Missouri in the
"constant . . . companionship of slaves, young and old, in this
community of cabins and small farms where the 'peculiar institution' of black servitude"[2] was maintained, took its toll. Discussing
the development of Twain's racial attitudes, Arthur G. Pettit
demonstrates that he began as a "conscious bigot,"[3] sharing the
orthodox Southern view of the Negro. Arriving in the North he was
alarmed by the Negro's social freedom; Justin Kaplan records one
of Twain's letters in which "with some anxiety he said that in a
hundred years there would be Negro supremacy in America, the
'whites under foot.' "[4] He confided to William Dean Howells that
he kept a Negro butler "because he did not like to give orders to a
white man."[5] If such views moderated into "more than anything,
ambivalence toward blacks," as Pettit points out, much of the
credit must go to the inhibiting influence imposed by Twain's
adopted Northeastern milieu.[6] But, as Helen L. Harris shows,
Twain was "unfailingly hostile"[7] toward the Indian too, and in

this respect the North provided few comparable restraining attitudes. Twain's vision of the Indian as ''treacherous, filthy, and repulsive,'' a vermin-eating beast, Satan's ''property,''[8] was free to grow in virulence. Twain felt little motivation to portray the red man objectively in his fiction. Moreover, the lack of inhibitions in regard to the Indian coupled with the repression of deep-seated hostility toward the Negro led to the emergence in Twain's work of the powerful Southern tendency to scapegoat the red man. Through the operation of the equation of black and red demonism Injun Joe, the red man who in the world of the novel is treated ''like a nigger!''[9] embodies an unmistakably powerful, double charge of racial disorder.

Few readers have failed to notice Injun Joe's diabolism. Lynn describes it as a quantity existing ''beyond—or below—the bounds of Heaven . . . across the limits of safety.'' ''Joe carries with him,'' Robert Tracy notes, ''the aura that surrounds the devil in legend.'' He is accused by Lewis Leary of being ''evil personified,'' seen by Leslie A. Fiedler as ''a threatening Satanic figure,'' ''the demonic guardian of the hoard''; he is the ''stuff,'' as Bernard DeVoto put it first, of ''ghosts and demons.''[10] Yet Joe is rarely granted the influence for disruption his demonic conception suggests. Normally *Tom Sawyer* is seen as benign, a uniformly ''charmed'' narrative, kept remote, in James M. Cox's words, ''like the 'once upon a time' of the fairy tale,'' by the enchanting perspective of a narrator whose existence depends upon an ''indulgence [which] is none other than the pleasure he takes in disclosing the play world.''[11] Narrative distance, not a surprising characteristic of an author whose ''entire genius—the 'Mark Twain' in Samuel Clemens—had his being in the tall tale,''[12] is made to account for the innocuous view of *Tom Sawyer*.

In the Southern tall tale or novel, however, nothing is more uncertain than ''indulgence'' in regard to the expression of the Negro or Indian. As has been seen in works like Johnson Jones Hooper's ''The 'Tallapoosy Vollantares' Meet the Enemy,'' a tale in the collection from which Twain may have borrowed the camp meeting episode in *Huckleberry Finn,* the good humor basic to narrative detachment quickly vanishes when the narrator encounters savage violence. The narrator of *Tom Sawyer* displays even less indulgence than Hooper's toward the Indian. At times he appears an Indian-hater, as when he condemns the "weaklings ready to scribble their names to a pardon-petition [for Injun Joe], and drip a tear on it from their permanently impaired and leaky water-works" (XII, 297). With its very existence predicated upon indulgence, the good-humored narrative voice virtually disappears in the episodes describing savage violence. Lacking the distance the voice provides, at these moments the narrative seems to move a step closer to expressing the underlying attitudes of the author.

In such situations, the narrator's voice is largely replaced by that of the character who by virtue of his persuasive capacity to create art seems at times to serve as a surrogate for the author himself. Stripped of the preoccupation with romantic adventure which Daniel G. Hoffman terms "imaginary baggage,"[13] the proximity of Tom Sawyer's point of view to the author's becomes unmistakable. Like the author, Tom possesses a sharply split artistic personality. He voices cosmic disorder, as when in a geography recitation he "turned lakes into mountains, mountains into rivers, and rivers into continents, till chaos was come again" (XII, 70-71). And he also excels at constructing visions of formally ordered conventionality, for example, luring Becky Thatcher with his sketch of "a house with two gable ends to it and a corkscrew of smoke issuing from the chimney," "a man in the front yard," and, in response to Becky's pleas, a girl—Becky herself—"coming along" (XII, 68-69). Most strikingly, Tom is an irresistible storyteller. In describing the graveyard murder, he compels total attention: "As he warmed to his subject his words flowed more and more easily; in a little while every sound ceased but his own voice; every eye fixed itself upon him; with parted lips and bated breath the audience hung upon his words, taking no note of time" (XII, 216). Just how close Tom does come to his author's vocation is suggested by the rhetoric into which the episode falls. The forms of legal testimony dissolve during Tom's narration, and for a moment judge, sheriff, lawyers, and spectators all seem transformed into "the audience" in an Old Southwestern humor anecdote, "rapt in the ghastly fascinations of the tale" (XII, 216).

What is seen during the moments in which Tom Sawyer describes Injun Joe are steps in the familiar sequence involving an initial eruption of demonic disorder followed by a relentless process of repression. Tom's conviction that the Indian is an implacably destructive devil, and the movement by which in his point of view the red man is increasingly depicted in highly formal settings serving to deny the figure its essential milieu of fantasy, places this narrative firmly in the tradition of demonic vision in Southern racial fiction. Indeed, the role played by the red man accounts for the presence of a narrative movement which, in spite of Twain's insistence that the novel is "strictly a history of a *boy*" (XII, 321), has led Leary and Walter Blair to suggest that *Tom Sawyer* ends with an approximation of adulthood for its boys.[14] As is found in the earlier fiction, a sense of rigidity, a harsh formality, overwhelms racial expression as it is swept by the repressive impulse directed at its demonic figure. Displaying this quality, the ending of *Tom Sawyer* is not so much adult in fact as adult by default. For as St. Petersburg is rid of the primordial threat posed by Injun Joe, it simultaneously loses its potential for the spontaneous fantasy associated with our vision of childhood. The ending of *Tom Sawyer* is still a children's world, but one characterized by the grim conventionality suggested by Tom's final complaint that its haunted houses are "all ripped up now" (XII, 319).

Injun Joe's initial appearance expresses the full extent of the demonic vision implicit in Twain's racial attitudes, a phenomenon unique in the narrative which results from the specific exigencies of plot involved in the graveyard murder episode. Twain makes use of the midnight scene to introduce the murderous Injun Joe subplot, and accordingly moves to evoke a melodramatic sense of apprehension appropriate to the heinous deed. He does so through manipulation of Tom's point of view, transforming it into a state suggesting nightmare by stripping it of the conscious sense of ordered time. Lying awake immediately before the nocturnal

adventure, Tom is at first unduly aware of mechanical time: "The
ticking of the clock began to bring itself into notice" (XII, 89). But
as Tom drowses, such abstract regularity modulates to a softer,
more natural rhythm: "Old beams began to crack mysteriously.
The stairs creaked faintly. . . . A measured, muffled snore issued
from Aunt Polly's chamber" (XII, 89). As the process continues,
Tom's point of view drifts further from consciousness: "And now
the tiresome chirping of a cricket that no human ingenuity could
locate, began" (XII, 89). The language of abstract time now
assumes a new definition, displaying a deathlike quality which
suggests how alien order has become to the point of view: "Next
the ghastly ticking of a death-watch . . . made Tom shudder"
(XII, 89). Finally all temporal perception is shed: "He was satisfied that time had ceased and eternity begun;. . . the clock chimed
eleven, but he did not hear it" (XII, 90), and the narrative enters
the state of "half-formed dreams" (XII, 90).

Predictably, in view of Tom Sawyer's potential proximity to the
narrative's underlying attitudes, this subjective state of vision
brings with it a mode of expression far more fundamental than
conventional melodrama. Already stripped of much of its defensive objectivity, Tom's point of view is brought into contact with
the racial violence guaranteed to breach the remaining component
of narrative detachment. A suggestion of the level of expression
toward which the narrative is moving is felt in the disembodied
warning that accompanies Tom's departure for the graveyard, a
sudden "cry of 'Scat! you devil!' " (XII, 90). Once within the
formless fluidity of the place—the graveyard is marked by "a
crazy board fence . . . which leaned inward in places, and outward the rest of the time, but stood upright nowhere. . . . Round-
topped, worm-eaten boards staggered over the graves, leaning for
support and finding none" (XII, 90-91)—Tom's vision becomes
expressive of a mode of fantasy which in its grimness shares
nothing of childish play. Now appearing, Injun Joe is a figure
directly in the tradition of Southern racial demonism, displaying
far more of the familiar diabolical characteristics than seem indicated by the exigencies of melodrama. First a voice which

"floated up from the far end of the graveyard" (XII, 92), Joe emerges amidst the fire-imagery that characterizes the demonic figure, the center of "innumerable little spangles of light" which is immediately identified as "devil-fire" (XII, 93). His eyes, notably without their well-known patch, like those of the earlier figures are "flaming with passion" (XII, 95). And when his malevolence erupts into action, when he "sprang to his feet, . . . snatched up Potter's knife, and went creeping, catlike and stooping, round and round about the combatants" (XII, 95), his implacable destructiveness is directly attributed to his racial origin, in a manner which reveals the darkness of Twain's underlying attitudes toward the red man. Displaying the qualities associated with demonic vision in the South, about to murder the young white doctor, Injun Joe is made to account for himself with an oath derived from one of the ugliest white racial stereotypes: "The Injun blood ain't in me for nothing" (XII, 95).

But the episode of demonic expression does not end here. At the graveyard the following day with most of the town, Tom's point of view still controls the narrative: Tom "turned, and his eyes met Huckleberry's" (XII, 110); "now Tom shivered from head to heel; for his eye fell upon the stolid face of Injun Joe" (XII, 110). And in the presence of the red man it displays the fluidity first noted during the previous night's description—"everything was swimming before Tom" (XII, 113)—indicating that vision is still sensitized to the expression of demonic associations. "Confirmed in [the] belief that Joe had sold himself to the devil" (XII, 112), the potential for influence upon the narrative by the attitudes Tom expresses suddenly becomes clear. Unlike the townspeople's perspective, Tom's surreal point of view accounts for the incident in which as "Injun Joe helped to raise the body of the murdered man and put it in a wagon for removal . . . it was whispered through the shuddering crowd that the wound bled a little!" (XII, 112-13), an event which the population interprets as confirming Muff Potter's guilt. The significant fact here is not so much that through Tom's point of view a surreal image is again expressed, but that the diabolical phenomenon now displays an ambiguous reality. In this last steps of the demonic eruption, Injun Joe's devilish attributes display a force which sharply pierces the narrative distance and gives them a virtual substantiality in terms of narrative action.

After the graveyard episode, however, the presence of Injun Joe temporarily fades from the narrative. The sense of demonic threat does not entirely vanish—it is occasionally alluded to in a grim rhetoric which jars sharply with the idyllic descriptions of the narrative: it is "a chronic misery. It was a very cancer for permanency and pain" (XII, 205). But the fear of the Indian is moderated, apparently because the red figure's destructiveness is not at first directed toward the crucial point of view, that of Tom himself. Such a direct relationship does not come into effect until the episode of the murder trial, when Tom testifies against the red man, thereby making himself a focus for the Indian's malevolence.

The courtroom scene, at the same time as focusing the danger upon the protagonist, also presents a sense of the process by which the racial disorder will be repressed. In transforming the courtroom into a recreation of the dreamlike milieu of the midnight graveyard, Tom's artistry makes clear the inverse relationship between the demonic figure's destructive energy and a formally structured context. Before Tom begins to testify, the courtroom reflects the highest degree of order; a place of legal "details" (XII, 213), its structured formality renders the demonic figure quiescent, "stolid" (XII, 212), like "iron" (XII, 215). As Tom tells his tale, however, and the setting increasingly reflects the fluid timelessness of the earlier episode, as "the audience hung upon his words, taking no note of time" (XII, 216), violence stirs in the red man. At first it is hardly noticeable: "A contemptuous smile flitted across Injun Joe's face" (XII, 215); "Injun Joe gave a barely perceptible start" (XII, 215). Yet with the setting reduced to a subjective fluidity, and Tom's point of view in intimate conjunction with his author's by virtue of its narrative artistry, a situation congenial to the expression of the Indian's demonic associations again occurs. Joe, his primordial energy seen in an image once more related to his dark racial origins, becomes momentarily irresistible: "Crash! Quick as lightning the half-breed sprang for a window, tore his way through all opposers, and was gone!" (XII, 216).

From this moment the narrative moves to block all expressions of the subjective state congenial to the depiction of the demonic figure by excluding from Tom's point of view the disordered fluidity of darkness. It transforms the quality of "nights [which] were seasons of horror [where] Injun Joe infested all his dreams, and always with doom in his eye" (XII, 217) into a function of his ordered daytime world illuminated with "splendor and exultation" (XII, 217). The process is seen at work in the next episode involving Injun Joe. Tom and Huck are on another playful search for mystery, this time for buried treasure. They agree that the most likely location to find it is in a haunted house. Only now the narrative explicitly avoids allowing the subjective abandon seen in the midnight milieu of the graveyard episode; here the boys are careful to approach the house "in the daytime," when spirits "don't come around" (XII, 228). In fact, subjectivity in the setting is further hedged against; even at noon on the first visit the setting seems questionable, for the boys remember that "a body can't be too careful. . . . We might 'a' got into an awful scrape, tackling such a thing on a Friday. . . . There's some lucky days, maybe, but Friday ain't" (XII, 229).

When Tom and Huck finally do enter the house, on "Saturday, shortly after noon . . . under the baking sun" (XII, 231), they find themselves in a context which is decrepit but formally structured, "a weed-grown, floorless room, unplastered, an ancient fireplace, vacant windows, a ruinous staircase" (XII, 232). It is a haunted house purged of its potential for the irrational; a place, for example, containing "a closet that promised mystery, but the promise was a fraud—there was nothing in it" (XII, 232). This setting is clearly uncongenial for the demonic figure, a situation which is reflected in Injun Joe's first exclamation upon entering the place: "What's more dangerous than coming here in the daytime!" (XII, 234). "Danger" for this figure of fantasy surely has a figurative meaning. Less than physical threat, it involves the symbolic effects of the repressive process that is underway in the narrative. Danger for Injun Joe means the suppression of his demonic attributes, a phenomenon which here is apparent in the first glimpse of the figure. For the very source of Joe's diabolical associations, his Indianness, is masked, concealed in the form of an "old deaf and dumb Spaniard. . . . Wrapped in a *serape;* he had bushy white whiskers; long white hair flowed from under his sombrero, and he wore green goggles" (XII, 233). Age and weakness dominate the appearance of the demonic figure in this structured environment: his once "flashing" eyes are hidden by "goggles"; his powerful body is enveloped in layers of heavy clothing. But the malevolent content of the figure too shows signs of being undercut. In the daylight Joe wants only to sleep: "Yawning, . . . Injun Joe said: 'I'm dead for sleep!'. . . . He curled down in the weeds and soon began to snore. His comrade stirred him once or twice and he became quiet" (XII, 234). And even with nightfall, as the setting begins to show some signs of the old subjectivity with Tom's sense that "time must be done and eternity growing gray" (XII, 235), the Indian's destructive energy seems sharply lessened. Joe stirs, in spite of his goggles "a wicked light flamed in his eyes" (XII, 238); spying the boys' digging tools he ascends the stairs to wreak destruction, but his malevolence is thwarted by the very objects of structural order with which he is being opposed. For "there was a crash of rotten timbers and Injun Joe landed on the ground amid the *débris* of the ruined stairway" (XII, 239). Blocked in this manner, Joe shows little trace of his old implacable evil. Instead the demonic figure seems irresolute: "He gathered himself up. . . . [He] grumbled awhile, . . . [and finally] slipped out of the house in the deepening twilight" (XII, 239).

Joe appears next in an even more formally structured context, a room in the Temperance Tavern. Here he is completely passive; Tom sees him simply "lying there, sound asleep on the floor, with his old patch on his eye and his arms spread out" (XII, 248). How far the repression of the demonic figure has progressed at this point is seen in a new quality which now appears in Tom's vision of the Indian. The boy describes Joe lying amidst "a bottle and a tin cup

on the floor . . . and lots more bottles in the room'' (XII, 249).
While Joe still seems a threat to Tom, his image now also suggests
a form of racial expression which is the polar opposite of demonic
vision. Through Tom's eyes Joe has come to seem as much
''drunk, I reckon'' (XII, 248), as demonic. His formidable
demonic energy on its way to elimination from the narrative, the
vision of Injun Joe has come to include the degrading stereotype of
the drunken Indian.

This glimpse of a prostrate Injun Joe is in fact the last sight of the
demonic figure before the episode in McDougal's Cave. Joe and
his friend are encountered once by Huck Finn, but significantly
here he is simply ''invisible'' (XII, 257), ''hidden in the gloom''
(XII, 257), perceived only as ''a voice—a very low voice'' (XII,
258). The Indian seems hardly to exist in Huck's point of view.
The only substantial realization the demonic figure has is in the
point of view of Tom, and that vision now firmly reflects the
narrative swing toward repression.

Why then does the final scene present the demonic figure in a
milieu surpassing even the midnight graveyard in its absence of
structured boundaries, an immense cave? Apparently the
McDougal Cave setting is a concession, as Blair suggests, to the
requirements of the melodramatic ''literary influences [which]
also operated''[15] in the depictions of Injun Joe. Twain himself
describes Injun Joe's starvation in the cave scene as enacted ''to
meet the exigencies of romantic literature.''[16] The description of
the cave does abound with conventional rhetoric. Entering the
cave is ''romantic and mysterious'' (XII, 254); it is a place of
''romantic'' ''adventures'' (XII, 256). The narrator himself points
to the heightened melodramatic quality of its mystery; the ''wonders of the cave . . . [are] dubbed with rather overdescriptive
names, such as 'The Drawing-Room,' 'The Cathedral,' 'Aladdin's Palace,' and so on'' (XII, 276). Yet in drawing upon this
memory, Twain was dealing with a place which also had the
grimmest associations; the real McDougal's Cave contained a
body said to be the owner's young daughter preserved in alcohol.[17]
Moreover, its dimensions seem to defy consciousness:

One might wander days and nights together through its intricate tangle of rifts and chasms, and never find the end of the cave; . . . he might go down, and down, and still down, into the earth, and it was just the same—labyrinth under labyrinth, and no end to any of them. No man "knew" the cave. That was an impossible thing. (XII, 255)

This level of profound subjectivity was inextricably related to the cave in Twain's imagination. In summoning melodrama, Twain also evoked the novel's last moment of spontaneous fantasy.

In this milieu of primordial disorder, where every utterance of Tom's now predominantly ordered point of view is unmistakably alien, "turned" by "the far echoes . . . all to jeering laughter" (XII, 280), "dying out in the distance in a faint sound that resembled a ripple of mocking laughter" (XII, 279), sounding "so hideously that he tried it no more" (XII, 285), by all rights the demonic figure should thrive. Readers normally have seen Joe at this point as finally realizing his demonic conception. As Tracy puts it, "Deep in the cave, at the heart of its mystery, the figure of Injun Joe appears again, guarding a treasure like all the legendary dark malevolent figures who lurk in the earth—trolls, gnomes, kobolds."[18] When Tom encounters Joe in the depths of the cave, however, the red man displays not the expected malevolence but indecision and weakness: Tom "was vastly gratified the next moment, to see the 'Spaniard' take to his heels and get himself out of sight" (XII, 287). In external narrative terms, there is no explanation for the figure's failure to enact his usual destructiveness. The lack of conventional motivation at this point is in fact emphasized by the inadequacy of the logic with which Tom attempts to account for the phenomenon. Since the red man is "not twenty yards away" (XII, 287), Tom's "reasoning" surely falls short: "Tom wondered that Joe had not recognized his voice and come over and killed him for testifying in court. But the echoes must have disguised the voice. Without doubt, that was it, he reasoned" (XII, 287). Similarly, there is no logical explanation for the figure's retention of its cumbersome "Spanish" disguise, apparently including the blinding green goggles, in the total security of the lightless cave. Such phenomena are accountable only as the end results of the process of repression which has rendered the demonic expression powerless in content and obscure in form.

Lifeless, Injun Joe's description is overwhelmed by the stereotyped rhetoric which had first appeared during the glimpse of the inert red figure in the Temperance Tavern. He becomes "the hapless half-breed" (XII, 296), the "flitting human insect" (XII, 296), whose "longing eyes had been fixed, to the latest moment, upon the light and the cheer of the free world outside" (XII, 294). The once formidable figure of spontaneous fantasy atrophies into a clichéd tourist attraction more overblown than even the other conventional objects of melodrama with which the cave abounds: "To this day the tourist stares longest at that pathetic stone [that Joe hollowed] and that slow-dropping water when he comes to see the wonders of McDougal's cave. Injun Joe's cup stands first in the list of the cavern's marvels; even 'Aladdin's Palace' cannot rival it" (XII, 296). This "burst of eloquence," which Henry Nash Smith finds "quite out of keeping with the tone of the book," nevertheless does serve a purpose beyond demonstrating "that the narrator can produce the kind of associations held in esteem by the dominant culture."[19] This veritable orgy of cliché, including passages such as "that drop was falling when the Pyramids were new; when Troy fell. . . . It is falling now; it will still be falling when all these things shall have sunk down the afternoon of history, and the twilight of tradition, and been swallowed up in the thick night of oblivion" (XII, 295-96), constitutes the stylistic counterpart of the celebration which sweeps the town when the protagonist is secured from the demon's lair. By invoking the most hyperbolic form of rhetorical conventionality, the narrative confirms that spontaneous demonic expression indeed has been purged from *Tom Sawyer*.

The general sense of civilized order which characterizes the ending of *Tom Sawyer* often has been noted. But the full influence upon the narrative of the repression of demonic expression is not limited to the "conformity"[20] which the uses of the $12,000 treasure marks in the boys' world. Along with the disorder, darkness, the state that in his confession "I have been like the rest of the race—never quite sane in the night"[21] the author associated with fundamental irrationality, is also purged from the narrative. The last view of St. Petersburg is of a place without darkness, a world defined by unnaturally continual illumination. Tom and Becky are saved by light: Tom "glimpsed a far-off speck that looked like daylight. . . . If it had only happened to be night he would not have seen that speck of daylight and would not have explored that passage any more!" (XII, 290-91). Back home, "The village was illuminated; nobody went to bed again" (XII, 290). As Tom reveals his secret of the fortune, the Widow Douglass's "place was grandly lighted" (XII, 307). In this context Tom is surely justified in feeling "an abounding sense of relief and security" (XII, 294). Bringing with it a world of conclusively uniform convention, safety has been bought at a high price.

The fate of Huckleberry Finn demonstrates the grimmest effects of the transformation that has occurred in the narrative of *Tom Sawyer*. Unlike that of Tom, Huck's point of view has remained allied with disorder. Initially, in his opposition to the restraints of time and space, Huck even resembles Injun Joe. Like Joe, "Huckleberry came and went, at his own free will. . . . He could go fishing or swimming when and where he chose, and stay as long as it suited him; . . . he could sit up as late as he pleased" (XII, 60). And also like the Indian's, Huck's fluidity seems a threat to the ordered community. Momentarily discounting the narrative humor, the description of Huck might well be that of Injun Joe: he was "hated and dreaded . . . because he was idle and lawless and vulgar and bad. . . . [He constituted a] forbidden society" (XII, 60). Because of the common bond of disorder, Huck's expression is strangely tied with the Indian's.

Without the dark associations of racial danger stirred by Joe's Indian blood, however, Huck Finn's aura of liberation evokes a certain quality of fertility and lyricism. Initially, Huck is enveloped in images of flowering; his clothes are "in perennial bloom and fluttering with rags" (XII, 60). He displays an almost larger than life image which suggests the surreal quality of an embryonic nature-figure. Like the transcendent boy in Walt Whit-

man's "Out of the Cradle Endlessly Rocking," "with his bare feet
the waves, with his hair the atmosphere dallying,"[22] Huck too at
this early moment seems to unite the elements. "His hat . . . a
vast ruin with a wide crescent lopped out of its brim, . . . and the
fringed legs [of his trousers] dragg[ing] in the dirt" (XII, 60), in
vernacular form the boy's description links the moon-like "crescent" of his "vast" hat to the earth below.

The narrative of *Tom Sawyer* can ill-afford to lose this lyrical
quality. Yet as the repressive movement blocks the spontaneity of
context necessary to Injun Joe's thriving, it simultaneously under-
cuts Huck Finn's vitality. At the same time that the Indian is dying
in the cave, Huck too weakens radically. He is described as "white
and jaded—you ain't well a bit" (XII, 268), as "very, very sick!"
(XII, 274); he is "delirious with fever" (XII, 272). When he
recuperates he is still weak, complaining: "I can't walk more'n a
mile, Tom—least I don't think I could" (XII, 299). Recovered,
the formerly flowering figure is described in the brittle rhetoric
characteristic of Injun Joe's final portrayal: "Whithersoever he
turned, the bars and shackles of civilization shut him in and bound
him hand and foot" (XII, 315). Huck has reemerged into a world
which has been rendered inimical to his fundamental lyricism.
Apparently defining his aesthetic goal in *Tom Sawyer* as the
creation of an ordered, stable conventionality, Twain in his *Autobiography* describes the elimination of Injun Joe as done "in the
interest of art."[23] If that is so, Huck's final statement is indicative
of the sacrifice involved in the process. Regarding his return to
civilization he cries: "I'll stick to the widder till I rot, Tom" (XII,
320). In that fleeting hint of corruption, of adhesive decay now
characterizing the lyrical figure, the ending of *Tom Sawyer* suggests the results of turning art to the uses of repression.

Chapter Five

"A Prisoner of Style":
The Uses of Art in
Huckleberry Finn
and *Pudd'nhead Wilson*

Racial expression in *Huckleberry Finn* (1885) and *Pudd'nhead Wilson* (1894), the two major narratives in which Mark Twain deals with the black man, seems in polar contrast to that seen in his treatment of the Indian in *Tom Sawyer*. While in the earlier book there is no doubt of the innateness of Injun Joe's malevolence, the black characters in the later books are viewed analytically, and their behavior is attributed to distorted social conditions. Yet in spite of the author's objective approach in regard to the Negroes, a telling similarity exists between the outcomes of the three racial narratives. The black men suffer a fate which is hardly less destructive than the Indian's: Nigger Jim, Tom Driscoll, and Roxy ultimately are deprived of their self-hood, figuratively or literally sold down the river. In a manner more unmistakable for the humanistic intent, the very forms of these narratives are expressive of dark racial attitudes. As Henry Nash Smith suggests, "The slogan of 'the damned human race' that later became Mark Twain's proverb spelled the sacrifice of art to ideology."[1] In *Huckleberry Finn* and *Pudd'nhead Wilson,* art is subverted by its enlistment in the service of repression.

II

The presence of racial repression in *Huckleberry Finn* scarcely has been overlooked. Almost uniformly, readers have condemned the long episode at the Phelps plantation in which Jim, as Chadwick Hansen points out, is transformed into "a sub-human creature who feels no pain, . . . a flat, cheap type."[2] Normally this grim treatment is viewed as the result of factors external to the conception of the black man: the crisis in Huck's point of view when he adopts the "Northern conscience," as James M. Cox suggests,[3] the realization, in Henry Nash Smith's words, "that the vernacular values embodied in [the] story were mere figments of the imagination, not capable of being reconciled with social reality,"[4] "the unhappy truth . . . that the author," as Leo Marx holds, "having revealed the tawdry nature of the culture of the great valley, yielded to its essential complacency,"[5] Twain's "failure in the management of point-of-view."[6] Surely, however, a reversal in characterization as appalling as that in which Jim plummets, as Hansen demonstrates, from the "high role" to "the lower role,"[7] stems from a factor integral to the author's conception of the black man itself. If, as Henry Nash Smith observes, Twain "did not see clearly where he was going when he began to write," certainly one of his "discoveries . . . in meaning"[8] consists of the perception of a subjective content in the expression of the black man far beyond any previously recognized in his vision of the Negro. More than any secondary narrative condition, the sudden realization of the extent of the irrationality basic to his racial attitudes is responsible for the "madness" which, as Neil Schmitz suggests, "Twain so deviously exhibited at the end of *Huckleberry Finn.*"[9]

The impulse toward expressing demonic vision is evident early in *Huckleberry Finn,* as it was in *Tom Sawyer.* There is a sense of the black man's dark subjective associations in the initial episode involving Nigger Jim. The setting during which Huck and Tom encounter him reads like a lesser version of the graveyard scene in *Tom Sawyer:* it is night, the place reverberates with inarticulate warnings, "the wind was trying to whisper something to me, and I couldn't make out what it was, and so it made the cold shivers run over me,"[10] clock time is distant, "away off in the town" (XIII, 18). In this relaxed context, Jim presents just the merest hint of aggressiveness. Blocking the boys' play by physically interposing himself between them, he issues a challenge: "Say, who is you? Whar is you? Dog my cats ef I didn' hear sumf'n. Well, I know what I's gwyne to do: I's gwyne to set down here and listen tell I hears it agin" (XIII, 20-21). In fact, the black man displays a relationship with light not entirely dissimilar to Injun Joe's: "setting in the kitchen door, . . . a light behind him," "Miss Watson's big nigger" (XIII, 20) must have appeared virtually surrounded by a sort of halo.

But in this case the first of a combination of narrative factors tends to inhibit demonic expression. Here indentureship thwarts the Negro's primordial content; as Daniel G. Hoffman points out, "Jim in slavery is helpless before the dark powers."[11] Accordingly, the demonic associations are easily dispelled by a humorous sublimation of the immediate controlling response. Instead of enacting their initial impulse "to tie Jim to the tree" (XIII, 21), the boys "play something on" (XIII, 21) the black man, exchanging a five cent piece for some candles and hanging his hat on a tree. The result is sufficiently repressive, for it transforms the disturbing sense of Jim's diabolical overtones into the harmless humor of racial stereotype: "Afterwards Jim said the witches bewitched him and put him in a trance, and rode him all over the State, and then set him under the trees again, and hung his hat on a limb to show who done it" (XIII, 22). In fact, the very hint of supernatural capabilities for the Negro is undercut by the awareness of its prosaic source: "Jim always kept that five-center piece round his neck with a string, and said it was a charm the devil give to him with his own hands, and told him he could cure anybody with it and fetch witches whenever he wanted to just by saying something to it; but he never told what it was he said to it" (XIII, 22). It is only through the awareness of Jim's subsequent escape that the meaning of Huck's final observation becomes apparent: that "on account of having seen the devil and been rode by witches," Jim indeed is "most ruined for a servant" (XIII, 22).

On Jackson's Island Jim literally is a runaway slave, and the demonic attributess are more forcefully expressed. It is not so much that the river lends Jim its primordial energy, as Hoffman suggests,[12] as that the fluid context liberates powers innate in the black man. Huck is led to his lair by a sign of the devil, "a good-sized snake" (XIII, 64). He perceives the presence of the Negro first by "a glimpse of fire" (XIII, 66), and when Huck finally encounters him, Jim is integrally associated with flame: "He had a blanket around his head, and his head was nearly in the fire" (XIII, 66-67). Most significantly, the presence of this dark figure now stirs in Huck the nameless dread earlier associated with the demonic encounter. There is little humor in Huck's terror, his inability to "sleep much . . . somehow, for thinking" (XIII, 66). The "fantods" (XIII, 66)—as Marx points out, "slang for wild fantasies, such as are suffered in attacks of delirium tremens"[13]— he experiences upon first seeing the black man emphasize the depth of his fear.

Paradoxically, however, during even this section which, with Jim escaped and embarking upon his journey toward freedom, would seem most conducive to spontaneous racial expression, a lurking ambivalence in the narrative induces yet further inhibition. The determination upon liberating the black man stirs an unmistakable uneasiness; as Schmitz points out, "As long as Jim is headed toward Cairo, life on the raft is not particularly 'free and easy.' If anything, Twain demonstrates repeatedly the barriers between white and black consciousness."[14] Alone with the black man, Huck himself becomes the instrument of repression through a periodic display of the "controlling voice" which, as Alan Trachtenberg suggests, "remains in force, internalized and sublimated"; it "now hides in the mask" of the first-person narrator.[15] In various ways, in this period Huck serves to deflect demonic expression.

This phenomenon accounts for the striking hostility with which Huck responds to Jim's frightening appearance. Huck employs humor in a two-fold defensive reaction. He virtually forces the black man into the stereotyped role of inept darky financier, a degradation which further serves to disarm the surreal implications of Jim's capacity to predict the future. And he plays another prank on the Negro, placing a dead rattlesnake "on the foot of Jim's blanket, ever so natural, thinking there'd be some fun when Jim found him there" (XIII, 81). It is a grim joke, made far grimmer when the black man is bitten by the snake's mate. But the results are hardly accidental, for Huck has repressed his belief in an inevitably deadly outcome to the trick. Jim's near fatal injury amounts to an unconsciously destructive act on Huck's part; it is what "comes of my being such a fool as to not remember that wherever you leave a dead snake its mate always comes there and curls around it" (XIII, 81).

On the river, considerable time passes without a further incident involving Jim's subjective relationship. Yet the repressive reactions triggered by his few tentative displays of individuality are so inordinate that they too surely constitute the response to a threatening dimension in the black man's conception well beyond humanistic expression. Huck follows his concession that Jim "had an uncommon level head for a nigger" (XIII, 110), for example, by forcing him into the stereotyped role of darky illogicality so relentlessly in the discussion of "ole King Sollermun" and foreign languages that the boy is able to retract his estimate, concluding "I see it warn't no use wasting words—you can't learn a nigger to argue. So I quit" (XIII, 115). In the same way, the episode during which the fog, as Henry Nash Smith suggests, projects Huck's "impulse to deceive Jim,"[16] concludes with an image the very dreamlikeness of which indicates the depth of the wish it expresses. With the boy's point of view like "dreaming; and when things began to come back to me they seemed to come up dim out of last week" (XIII, 119), Huck expresses a vision in which the black man in a fetal position, no longer in control of the raft, displays the most primary helplessness: "When I got to it Jim was setting there with his head down between his knees, asleep, with his right arm hanging over the steering-oar" (XIII, 119). Such a heightening hostility, in sharp contradiction to the projection of objective racial attitudes, may have played a role in the temporary abandonment of the manuscript at this point.

Beyond Cairo, however, an inversion occurs in the narrative. With freedom for Jim no longer a possibility, the inhibiting uneasiness formerly evident in the narrative dissipates; as Hansen suggests, "One can sense [Twain's] relief once he gets Jim past Cairo and settled at the river's pace."[17] The extent of the narrative's relaxation of controls at this point is indicated by a curious inattention to plot details. As Marx points out, the initial purpose of the journey is so thoroughly forgotten that when the pair discover a canoe which would enable them to regain Cairo, there is not a thought of using it for Jim's liberation.[18] This unique indifference to form, together with the fluidity of the river at night, renders the narrative highly vulnerable to the spontaneous expression of demonic vision.

There is in fact an astonishing transformation in the attitudes toward Jim's surreal associations. Jim now seems a figure of primitive fecundity. Discovered at the end of the Grangerford episode deep in a swamp "very thick with trees and bushes and vines," "laying there asleep" in "a little open patch as big as a bedroom, all hung around with vines" (XIII, 153), he resembles nothing more than a dormant nature god. And when awakened, his powers easily transcend those of the "seer and shaman, interpreter of the dark secrets of nature which the white folks . . . cannot discover"[19] that Hoffman ascribes to him. This deific figure produces in a manner which far surpasses the literal probabilities of plot an almost magically reconstituted raft, and a meal of "corndodgers and buttermilk, and pork and cabbage and greens" beyond which "there ain't nothing in the world so good when it's cooked right" (XIII, 159-60). "Free and easy and comfortable" (XIII, 160) transportation and sumptuous food; surely Nigger Jim has become for the moment an image of irrational gratification, a vernacular American genie.

No wonder on the river at night, with clock time afar off on shore, Jim is able to give expression to his primordial content through a nature myth of cosmic dimensions, an irrational theory accounting organically for the very creation of the heavens: "We had the sky up there, all speckled with stars, and we used to lay on our backs and look up at them, and discuss about whether they was made or only just happened. . . . Jim said the moon could a *laid* them. . . . We used to watch the stars that fell, too, and see them streak down. Jim allowed they'd got spoiled and was hove out of the nest" (XIII, 163). Jim's myth is in polar opposition to the "literal-mindedness"[20] which Kenneth S. Lynn points out is fundamental to the point of view, the quality expressed when Huck counters with a skeptical view of the universe as a product of chance: "I allowed they happened; I judged it would have took too long to *make* so many" (XIII, 163). But in the "whole world of sparks" (XIII, 164) which, erupting out of the "chimbleys" of passing steamboats transforms the entire setting with the familiar demonic imagery of light, there is unmistakable evidence of the irresistible force underlying the black man's vision. In this understated but fundamental confrontation of first principles the Negro's view triumphs, and its unconscious, irrational basis undermines even the language of reason, putting it to the service of myth: Huck concludes that Jim's account "looked kind of reasonable, so I didn't say nothing against it" (XIII, 163).

In spite of its benign form, this vision of the black man has brought about a highly unstable situation, for in undermining Huck's normally literal point of view it poses a threat to the narrative integrity beyond any of his abortive grapplings with conscience. The narrative response is a measure of the magnitude of the crisis, the novel's greatest. Within bare seconds of reading time, with an urgent determination, the Duke and the King come "tearing up the path as tight as they could foot it. . . . [They] wanted to jump right in" (XIII, 164) Huck's canoe, to put an end to the river setting's provocatively easeful ambience. Their arrival, initiating the long process of repression that changes the entire tone of *Huckleberry Finn*, constitutes the familiar narrative reaction to the expression of demonic vision.

Indeed, there is a narrative change in this section which suggests just how fundamental the repression brought about by these two figures is to the novel. It is normally recognized that during this section the author draws uncomfortably close to the action; as Henry Nash Smith points out, "Mark Twain's satiric method requires that Huck be a mask for the writer, not a fully developed character."[21] Yet there also is a telling relationship between the author and the younger and more active of the pair of new characters. "Jour printer by trade, . . . [practicer of] phrenology when there's a chance, . . . sling a lecture sometimes" (XIII, 166), the Duke bears a striking resemblance to Mark Twain, himself a printer, phrenologist, and lecturer. It is no wonder that in each of his actions toward Nigger Jim the Duke employs the tools of the artist: inks, paints, brushes, and theatre constumes. In this general narrowing of narrative distance Huck may embody Twain's outrage at Southern society, but the Duke through his uses of art to repress the black man expresses the darker racial underside of the author's cultural attitudes.

Accordingly, the Duke's actions toward Jim, while ostensibly adhering to the resolution finally to liberate the black man which, as Victor Doyno demonstrates, existed long before the concluding scene,[22] in fact sharply intensifies the process of dehumanization figuratively destroying the Negro. The Duke's first act is to bind Jim, apparently using aesthetics in the name of humanity. By employing "ropes . . . the correct thing—we must preserve the unities, as we say on the boards" (XIII, 182), in order to increase Jim's resemblance to a captured slave, he decreases the possibility of the black man being taken by other slave hunters and indentured in fact. In the piece of art which makes the benevolence possible, however, there is evidence of the depersonalizing impulse at work. To justify the binding, the Duke prints a handbill, a "little job he'd printed and hadn't charged for, because it was for us. It had a picture of a runaway nigger with a bundle on a stick over his shoulder, and '$200 reward' under it. The reading was all about Jim, and just described him to a dot" (XIII, 181). In this primitive aesthetic creation, fixing the black man in the very act of escape, forcing him into the stereotyped form of "a runaway nigger," the long process transforming Jim, in Tom Sawyer's words, into "a prisoner of style" (XIII, 344), begins.

In the same way the Duke's response to Jim's complaint that "it got mighty heavy and tiresome to him when he had to lay all day in the wigwam tied with a rope" (XIII, 209) is apparently benevolent, freeing the black man through his transformation into the image of a "Sick Arab" frightening enough to keep away all intruders. Yet at the same time the act makes of the Negro a figure depersonalized to such an extent that Huck's observation, "Why, he didn't only look like he was dead, he looked considerable more than that" (XIII, 210), assumes a grimly symbolic meaning. The Duke's aesthetic creation serves as a paradigm of the uses to which the art of *Huckleberry Finn* has been put in regard to the black man: "He dressed Jim up in King Lear's outfit—it was a long curtain-calico gown, and a white horse-hair wig and whiskers; and then he took his theater paint and painted Jim's face and hands and ears and neck all over a dead, dull, solid blue" (XIII, 209). Employing the forms of Shakespearian art for antihumanistic purposes, surely Jim's repression holds the highest priority in the narrative. Enveloped by white wig and whiskers, the residue of his humanity eradicated by the injunction to "fetch a howl or two like a wild beast" (XIII, 210), Jim's primordial content predictably turns putrid, "like a man that's been drownded nine days" (XIII, 209).

Captivity at the Phelps plantation simply concludes the process of Jim's dehumanization begun on the river. By way of insuring the completeness of the black man's enervation before his freedom literally is conferred, *all* the forms of art are turned against him in a veritable fury of repression. Graphic art again is used aggressively, as in Tom Sawyer's design of Jim's coat of arms which, in a manner now far more formalized than the Duke's rudimentary handbill, captures Jim within the same stereotype of the escaped slave: "Crest, a runaway nigger, *sable,* with his bundle over his shoulder on a bar sinister" (XIII, 333). Music is used to heighten his degradation. In a vicious mockery of his liberation Tom advises Jim to "play your jews-harp; play 'The Last Link is

Broken' '' (XIII, 338), not by way of anticipating his coming freedom, but because ''that's the thing that'll scoop a rat quicker'n anything else; and when you've played about two minutes you'll see all the rats, and the snakes, and spiders, and things begin to feel worried about you, and come. And they'll just fairly swarm over you, and have a noble good time'' (XIII, 338). The written word too involves the wounding of Jim: ''Every time a rat bit Jim he would get up and write a little in his journal whilst the ink was fresh'' (XIII, 342). This image surpasses in significance Hansen's point that in it Jim has ''become a sub-human creature who feels no pain and bleeds fresh ink.''[23] Painfully, it symbolizes the process of aesthetic creation at the end of *Huckleberry Finn*. In it the act of writing transforms the black man's very existence into the lifeless printed word of a journal based on corrupt literary forms.

The image of Jim at the novel's conclusion, a black stereotype ''pleased most to death'' (XIII, 373) at Tom's forty dollar condenscension, realizes the narrative's goal. There is scarcely a distinction between this figure and the other stereotyped darkies, slaves like a ''yaller wench'' (XIII, 326), and Nat, who ''had a good-natured, chuckle-headed face'' (XIII, 305) upon which a smile spreads ''around graduly . . . like when you heave a brick-bat in a mud-puddle'' (XIII, 305), with whom the Phelps planta-tion abounds. The enervation of the black man, about to be freed, but helpless ''in [a] calico dress, with his hands tied behind him'' (XIII, 363), is unmistakable. Apparently intended as an expres-sion of his nobility, the speech in which Jim chooses slavery over freedom in order to help the wounded Tom Sawyer by its selfless abasement and in its exceptional emphasis upon simplified black dialect is a testimony to the Negro's final harmless insubstantial-ity: ''Ef it wuz *him* dat 'us bein' sot free, en one er de boys wuz to git shot, would he say, 'Go on en save me, nemmine 'bout a doctor f'r to save dis one?' Is dat like Mars Tom Sawyer? Would he say dat? You *bet* he wouldn't! *Well,* den, is *Jim* gwyne to say it? No, sah—I doan' budge a step out'n dis place 'dout a *doctor;* not if it's forty year!'' (XIII, 353). Even freed, there is no threat to the point of view from this source; Huck's final observation about Jim confirms the restoration of stability to the narrative's basic racial attitudes: "I knowed he was white inside, . . . so it was all right now" (XIII, 353).

Turned to such antihumanistic ends, the narrative loses its capacity for lyricism. The shift in tone occurring soon after the appearance of the Duke and the King is manifested by the descriptions of Arkansas, in which, as Lynn points out, "images of whiteness have been replaced by images of blackness and filth; gardens no longer bloom."[24] Yet this transformation of the formerly fecund setting into a place of "jimpson-weeds, and sunflowers, and ash piles, and old curled-up boots and shoes, and pieces of bottles, and rags, and played-out tinware" (XIII, 187) seems almost innocuous compared to the quality which overcomes the book as the process of repression nears its conclusion. For finally, on the Phelps plantation, Aunt Sally's voice comes to dominate the novel's language, and its propensity for malapropism constitutes a meduim through which is expressed the full corruption resulting from the distortion of art. Perceived through the voice of this character who describes herself as "most putrified" (XIII, 298), narrative data are transformed into disease, as in her initial description of a case in which "mortification set in, and they had to amputate him. But it didn't save him. Yes, it was mortification—that was it. He turned blue all over" (XIII, 287). Allowed one of the novel's rare external descriptions of the first-person narrator, Aunt Sally's unique vision gives a vivid reality to Huck's acknowledgement of the taint upon his creative role: "There ain't nothing more to write about, and I am rotten glad of it" (XIII, 374). In her translation of the "streak of butter [that] come a-trickling down [his] forehead" (XIII, 349) during a prank into a vernacular image of the narrator's terminal mental disease, "the brain-fever as shore as you're born, and they're oozing out!" (XIII, 349), there is a definitive confirmation of the full extent to which racial repression has corrupted the imaginative impulse underlying the narrative of *Huckleberry Finn*.

III

In contrast to the sense of malaise which overwhelms the ending of *Huckleberry Finn*, with the condemnation of Tom Driscoll a well-being beyond even the brittle celebration capping *Tom Sawyer* sweeps *Pudd'nhead Wilson*. It is not surprising that for this figure from whose "character," as Henry Nash Smith puts it, there are "intimations of evil radiating,"[25] there is no sense of loss in the narrative. In spite of the attempts to account for his behavior sociologically as the product of his " 'training' [as] a white slaveholder with the white slaveholder's vices,"[26] in Stanley Brodwin's words, there is finally little sympathy in the conception of this malevolent black murderer. But, as Tom Driscoll is purged from the narrative, at the same time his mother is destroyed: "Roxy's heart was broken. . . . The spirit in her eye was quenched, . . . the voice of her laughter ceased in the land. In her church and its affairs she found her only solace."[27] And, if the narrative directs unrelieved hatred toward Tom, the author's sympathies with this partly black woman, "shapely, intelligent, and comely—even beautiful" (XIV, 23), are clear. Why then, if not for Tom, is there no trace of remorse at Roxy's grim fate? For with her repression the narrative is rid of the "magic power," "the unconscious power she commands,"[28] as Cox puts it, which, expressed through "her martial bearing" (XIV, 224), makes of Roxy the narrative's source of demonic racial vision.

With Roxy, however, the expression of demonic vision takes an unfamiliar form. If not imprisoned literally, or through racial stereotype, Roxy is nevertheless the captive of the stereotype of her sex. There is a sense of the limitations her femininity posed for the Victorian author in the episode during which she recounts her escape from slavery on the Arkansas plantation. It is only when transformed into a black *man* through the disguise of "shabby old clothes, sodden with rain . . . [with which she] showed a black face under an old slouch hat" (XIV, 167-68), that Roxy sheds the delicacy of womanhood sufficiently to be allowed to describe "all de hell-fire dat 'uz ever in my heart [which] flame' up, [when she] snatch de stick outen [her overseer's] han' en laid him flat'' (171). Inhibited in such a manner, the manifestations of Roxy's demonic impulses are forced into the traditional patterns of the female stereotype. Apparently a passive figure, the "aggressive consequences"[29] that Cox finds in her actions are predictable. It is by the sublimation of her dark impulse through the creation of a proxy free to enact destructiveness in the white world that Roxy's demonic content erupts.

The import of the subjective associations evidenced as Roxy exchanges her partly black male baby for the Driscoll family's rightful white heir, thereby releasing it into an unsuspecting society, is clear. In the traditional manner, the narrative seems swept by a sense of intense unconsciousness: "she seemed in a trance," "she began to move about like one in a dream" (XIV, 33). Roxy herself displays a diabolical quality barely limited by its sensuous femininity: dressed in "a conflagration of gaudy colors and fantastic figures" (XIV, 31), she becomes "her own volcanic irruption of infernal splendors" (XIV, 32). But this image of demonic vision pales in contrast to the eruption expressed at the point at which, with her son mature and capable of substantial action, she completes the establishment of his black identity. In "the haunted house" (XIV, 82), a setting much as in *Tom Sawyer* emphasizing the supernatural, Roxy sits as if on "a throne" (XIV, 86) under the familiar "tin lantern freckling the floor with little spots of light" (XIV, 83) suggesting demonic energy. Performing her sublimated act of malevolence, setting Tom up as her surrogate prowler by informing him "You's a *nigger!—bawn* a nigger en a *slave!*" (XIV, 84), her eyes reveal the same fiery malignancy as Injun Joe's during his murder of Doctor Robinson: "Her eyes flamed with triumph" (XIV, 83). Surely Tom's last expression before he succumbs to his blackness stands as the white evaluation of Roxy's role: reacting to her insistence, "Yassir—you's my *son*" (XIV, 84), he cries "You devil!" (XIV, 84).

In response to his mother's eruption of demonic energy, Tom himself experiences "a gigantic eruption, like that of Krakatoa" (XIV, 90), a volcanic explosion of primordial dimensions which confirms his diabolical role. A telling characteristic of the forms of Tom's demonic expression makes its source clear: serving as a surrogate for a darker woman's malevolent impulses, there is a confusion in both Tom's color and his sex. The blurring of his male, seemingly white, identity is anticipated in the image of the double which parodies his aristocratic surface: "When Tom started out on his parade next morning he found the old deformed negro bell-ringer straddling along in his wake tricked out in a flamboyant curtain-calico exaggeration of his finery, and imitating his fancy Eastern graces as well as he could" (XIV, 50). The derivation of Tom's identity becomes unmistakable as his actions grow more destructive: setting out on "his raid" (XIV, 94), he carries "a suit of girl's clothes with him in a bundle . . . and was wearing a suit of his mother's clothing, with black gloves and veil" (XIV, 94). And when he murders his adopted white father, as Cox points out, "disguised as a Negro when he plunges the Indian knife into the Judge's heart,"[30] Tom first "got his suit of girl's clothes out . . . and laid it by" (XIV, 185), so that after this surpassingly destructive act he can assume his full identity as surrogate for the deadly woman.

An entirely symbolic figure with scarcely an identity of his own, Tom's actions are capable of conveying the full subjective charge of demonic destructiveness. Tom's murder of his adopted father is no less an expression of evil than Injun Joe's stabbing of Dr. Robinson. The rhetoric describing this eruption is virtually identical to that of the episode in the earlier novel: "Without hesitation he drove the knife home—and was free" (XIV, 186). Indeed, in Roxy's fantastic genealogy there is a mixture of red and black blood which suggests Tom's function as a symbolic combination of the malevolence associated with the two races: "My great-great-great-gran'father en yo' great-great-great-great-gran'father was Ole Cap'n John Smith, de highest blood dat Ole Virginny ever turned out, en *his* great-great-gran'mother or somers along back dah, was Pocahontas de Injun queen, en her husbun' was a nigger king outen Africa" (XIV, 139).

In response to such an extreme expression of demonic vision, the narrative of *Pudd'nhead Wilson* is fairly overwhelmed by the impulse to reestablish order. The role of repressing the black figures is filled by David Wilson, after whom the novel significantly is named. His means of effecting the black man's imprisonment are based on the most relentlessly ordering techniques of late nineteenth-century science, the analytical process of ascertaining human identity through fingerprinting. It is by this skill, a manifestation of his character, as Henry Nash Smith puts it, "incarnate analytical intelligence, the personification of science,"[31] that Wilson dispels the subjective context necessary for the demon's expression, as he "began to shred away" "unconsciousness" (XIV, 205). Through it he arrives at an objective perception which gives a new and strikingly dark meaning to the traditionally inspirational phrase: "Heavens, what a revelation!" (XIV, 205). For working as a technician of the Gilded Age ought, "under a high pressure of steam" (XIV, 206) to establish "a plan in which a progressive order and sequence was a principal feature" (XIV, 207), Wilson uncovers the dark relationship between Roxy and Tom Driscoll which gives the narrative's demonic energy its substance.

It is fitting, therefore, that the narrative concludes with the trial, the culmination of the detective story plot line with which, as Leslie A. Fiedler points out, the "universal guilt and doom," the "tragic inevitability" of the novel "is crossed."[32] The ending of *Pudd'nhead Wilson* has nothing whatever to do with its humanistic beginning. Once the destructiveness of demonic vision has been loosed in the narrative, the restoration of order attains the highest priority. The novel becomes obsessed with the elimination of the Negro's capacity for independent action, not the establishment of his humanity. It is toward the final image of Tom, encompassed by the implacable forms of legal repression, "growing limp [as] the life seemed oozing out of him" (XIV, 221) that, as Twain himself insisted, the narrative of *Pudd'nhead Wilson* moves "straight ahead without divergence."[33]

Chapter Six

The Limits of Humanity in the Fiction of William Faulkner

By the 1930s and early 1940s attitudes toward the Negro and the Indian in the South had drifted far apart. In this period the first real seeds of liberal thought about the black man took root in the Southern consciousness. In regard to the Negro, Civil Rights issues had begun to be confronted on an everyday basis, and the question of the black man's changing role assumed a new meaning for the Southern white. At the same time the Indian had become eclipsed in Southern awareness. Removal had been accomplished over a century earlier, and with scant exceptions the red man was unknown in the South. Decades would pass before his plight became a significant social issue. Accordingly, the great part of the Southerner's perception of the red man came from earlier writings rather than direct observation or current thought. In a perhaps inevitable way the Indian largely had lost his place in the foreground of the Southern imagination.

This situation established a potential in Southern fiction for the polarization of the vision of the Negro and Indian. While the conflict between the new humanitarianism and powerful traditional attitudes offered substance to a vital depiction of the black man, both the quantity and nature of writings about the red man withered. Both conditions are best expressed in the works of William Faulkner; Faulkner's fiction offers the most recent major statement of the role of the Negro and Indian in the Southern imagination. For if Faulkner excels at depicting the painful struggle involved in seeing the black man objectively, he also reveals through scattered tales the implications for Southern fiction of viewing the Indian, as Arthur F. Kinney suggests in the case of Sam Fathers, as "a relic, superannuated."[1]

Nowhere in Faulkner's descriptions of the Indian is the meaning of superannuation better expressed than in an early tale, "Red Leaves." While this story will be discussed more extensively in regard to its black protagonist, its depiction of the red man reveals a whole new spectrum of characteristics suggesting the profound alteration in the traditional conception of the Indian. In contrast to the potential for engulfment by unbounded disorder often posed by earlier savage figures, the red men in this tale are seen with a definitive remoteness, displaying the unmistakable abstractness of two-dimensional perspective. Expressing, in Lewis M. Dabney's words, "the survival of the archaic within the Southern scene,"[2] they are like museum pieces, bas reliefs with their "big heads, big, broad, dust-colored faces of a certain blurred serenity like carved heads on a ruined wall in Siam or Sumatra." The lifeless stasis of artifact dominates their description: "Upon [the chief's] supine monstrous shape there was a colossal inertia, something profoundly immobile, beyond and impervious to flesh."[3] Flat, still; beyond the "monstrous shape" of the red man there now seems to lie only imaginative enervation.

This shift in the basis of the vision of the Indian accounts for the elusiveness underlying Faulkner's greatest depiction of the red man, Sam Fathers. While Sam Fathers is of mixed red and black ancestry, his Indianness is dominant. He is seen with "the Indian face above the nigger clothes."[4] In "The Old People" and "The Bear" he is consciously related to the vital primordial forces shared by the savage: he is "a wild man . . . [who] knew things that had been tamed out of our blood so long ago that we have not only forgotten them, we have to live together in herds to protect ourselves from our own sources."[5] He is given the surreal power of the supernatural red figure; Sam Fathers is capable of clairvoyance: "It had been foreknowledge in Sam's face that morning."[6] He is physically strong, as his taming of the giant dog Lion suggests. Nevertheless, in spite of Faulkner's attempt to endow this Indian with a content of primordial energy, there is an inescapable weakness in the image. Described sporadically in terms of depletion similar to those seen in "Red Leaves," Sam Fathers, "alien" and "barren,"[7] of a "vanished"[8] people, "motionless,"[9] shares the subjective exhaustion underlying Faulkner's expression of the red man.

The effects of this uncertainty in the conception of the Indian are felt as an overall narrative ambivalence in these two stories and a third, "Delta Autumn," which make up a wilderness trilogy. While readers have been aware of an ambivalence in the outcome of the trilogy, in which the white protagonist, Isaac McCaslin, dies embodying only a barren celibacy, "uncle to half a county and still father to none, living in one small cramped fireless rented room,[10] they have tended to place the source in a flaw in Isaac's characterization. Francis Lee Utley, for example, suggests that "perhaps there is some deficiency in this [white] hunter, initiated into a man's world.[11] Kinney speaks of Isaac's "self-righteousness and . . . tawdry moral superiority."[12] Yet in the sequence the white is dependent upon the Indian for the vitality in his world view, for in the first two tales it is to Sam Fathers that Isaac McCaslin goes for the vision of primordial purity upon which he bases his life. The vision must be communicated on a subjective level; it is of a nature to preclude articulation. As T. H. Adamowski maintains, "What Ike receives from Sam is an image of the wilderness."[13] It is this very component of Faulkner's conception of the Indian, the implicit subjective vitality traditionally associated with the savage, which is most in question. What appears a deficiency in the conception of Isaac is in fact a function of the subjective enervation underlying Faulkner's vision of Sam Fathers, for Isaac can only receive a hollow communion from the red man. The barrenness of Isaac McCaslin is a gauge of the decline in the Indian's primordial tradition.

Amidst the complexity of Faulkner's treatment of the Indian there is after all little attempt to depict the red man realistically. In one manner or another, as Utley points out in the case of Sam Fathers, the Indian's role is "symbolic."[14] This is not so in

Faulkner's depiction of the black man. Readers have long acknowledged, with Robert Penn Warren, that Faulkner has striven "to make the [black] character transcend his sufferings *qua* Negro to emerge to us not as Negro but as man."[15] Irene Edmonds, for example, refers to Faulkner's move toward "unspoken recognition of the subtle intricacies of the personalities of his Negro characters, . . . [his] silent tribute to their basic human reserve and dignity."[16] But this objective impulse is not so easily realized in Faulkner's writings. The fact that stereotyped racial characters frequently appear in Faulkner's fiction is evidence of the influence upon the author of traditional Southern racial attitudes. Characters such as Dilsey in *The Sound and the Fury* (1929), Philadelphy in *The Unvanquished* (1938), and Nancy Manigoe in *Requiem for a Nun* (1951), for example, all display the two-dimensional quality attributed in the dedication of *Go Down, Moses* to Caroline Barr, who "gave to [Faulkner's] family a fidelity without stint or calculation or recompense and to [his] childhood an immeasurable devotion and love." As Walter Taylor points out, "The most obvious thing about each of these figures is its traditional nature. Dilsey and Nancy are both 'mammies' whose chief source of identification is the white family they serve; their very heroism is a kind of subservience."[17] In the light of such dehumanized characterizations, it seems likely that, as Taylor convincingly demonstrates, "Faulkner's feelings toward blacks were never more than ambivalent,"[18] that, in Ralph Ellison's words, in regard to the Negro "Faulkner's attitude is mixed."[19]

The fictional price of such ambivalence is felt most strongly when Faulkner tries to depict the black man without stereotype. Faulkner's humanistic expressions of Negroes always involve struggle, depend upon violence. It may be, as Charles H. Nilon suggests, that for Faulkner the expression of black humanity revolves about the Negro's victimization by whites:

> As victims, these characters are usually morally superior to their oppressors. Many of them achieve victories through defeat. In most of the stories there is a chase motif in which the Negro character may use flight or evasion as a means of survival. The chase usually ends

with the physical annihilation of the character but it frequently is made to symbolize the character's moral victory.[20]

But more likely it is the violence itself, the crime, which plays the central role. Faulkner, through his capacity to identify with the minds of his Negro characters, intuited that for the black man, in Taylor's words, "to gain his humanity, it appears necessary to assume, however unconsciously, the responsibility for violating conventional morality."[21] Violence is the black man's human response, as Eldridge Cleaver has pointed out, to his sense of being dehumanized. In Faulkner's writings, black disorder defines black humanity.

Yet in the imagination of an author who, as Irving Howe suggests, shares the "deeper phobias of the folk mind,"[22] black disorder is also guaranteed to stir the spectre of racial demonism. An agonizing paradox results in these expressions of the Negro in which Faulkner's modern sense of the black man's grim realities brings about an inevitable conflict with his irrational inherited racial attitudes. Inescapably, the situation influences Faulkner's writings, for as the black man's desperate violence evokes a sense of the surreal, the traditional repressive reaction against demonic racial disorder becomes felt in the narrative. At best, such defensive impulses remain in an uneasy equilibrium with the author's humanistic attitudes toward the Negro. In extreme situations, the narrative swings more sharply toward repression. Always, irresolution characterizes the narratives of Faulkner's most candid expressions of the black man, adding another dimension to Alfred Kazin's suggestion that Faulkner does not always succeed "in his attempt to will his painful material into a kind of harmony that it does not really possess."[23]

An early expression of this phenomenon is seen in the case of the Negro in "Red Leaves." As has been discussed, the Indian in this story appears static and remote, the imaginative foundation of his portrait exhausted. But the Negroes with whom the story deals, slaves kept by the Indian tribe, contrast sharply in giving evidence of a complex unconscious vitality in their conception. Glimpsed, for example, in their dark cabin, the black men seem "like the roots of a huge tree uncovered, the earth broken momentarily upon the writhen, thick, fetid tangle of its lightless and outraged life.''[24] In a stable context such implicit substance in black characterization lies hidden, buried beneath a surface which appears in one image of ordinary slaves as a double barrier: "the thoughts sealed inscrutable behind faces like the death masks of of apes" (117). The effect is that in unexceptional situations the complexity of Negro characterization is simply inaccessible; the black men appear as all stereotype. Normally in this story they "prefer sweating" (102), are "savages" (104), live "in utter idleness" (107), and are "shiftless slaves" (107).

It is only when one black man is forced to act, in this case the nameless body servant of the dying Indian chief who is driven to attempt escape in the face of his impending funeral sacrifice, that the implicit content becomes realized. Before fleeing, this Negro seems particularly hollow; he is "the one who held the pot" (115) for twenty-three years of servitude. Yet in running from his owners his description takes on a new, concrete quality: he becomes "the Negro gaunt, lean, hard, tireless and desperate" (124). His character becomes dominated by an increasing internal complexity. Self-awareness occurs in a dramatically basic form; for the first time he comes to understand his own will to live: "Then he said it again—'It's that I do not wish to die'—in a quiet tone, of slow and low amaze, as though it were something that, until the words had said themselves, he found that he had not known, or had not known the depth and extent of his desire" (124). At the last, just before his capture, the Negro's brief rebellion flowers into a poignant moment of overt self-expression: "He began to sing. . . . He was chanting something in his own language, his face lifted to the rising sun. His voice was clear, full, with a quality wild and sad" (128). During his escape a qualitative difference separates the protagonist from those Negroes who have not defined themselves through an act against established morality. On fleeing he passes another black man, and "the two men, the one motionless and the other running, looked for an instant at each other as though across an actual boundary between two different worlds" (120).

As the black's characterization grows in substance in response to his act of self-assertion, the threatening associations of Negro rebellion stir a familiar strain of imagery in the narrative. The traditionally dark Southern racial attitudes are muted in "Red Leaves," since in this tale Indians are surrogates for white slave holders. Nevertheless, they are discernible in the view of the black presented as his rebelliousness is taking form. The slave is hidden in a barn, preparing to flee at this master's death: "He had a flat nose, a close, small head; the inside corners of his eyes showed red a little, and his prominent gums were a pale bluish red above his square, broad teeth. He had been taken at fourteen by a trader off Kamerun, before his teeth had been filed" (116-17). The gratuitous assurance that apparently this slave was spared the uncivilized deformity of having his teeth filed to a point paradoxically introduces the very threat it denies, for it evokes the subliminal image of a savage black countenance with fiercely pointed teeth.

Certainly as he flees the Negro more overtly is seen in savage form. He casts off his "dungaree pants" (122), a token of his earlier harmlessly domesticated state, and coating "himself with mud—face, arms, body and legs" (122), is reincarnated in a grotesque image of an aborigine. Most tellingly, the black increasingly displays the images traditionally indicative of unconscious demonic associations. As his escape progresses, his eyes, which at first seemed merely red, come to radiate a surreal energy. In the early stages of the rebellion "his eyeballs were a little luminous" (117). They glow "with a quiet light" (120). Finally, when the Negro's rebellion is clearly irreversible, his eyes come to seem the outlet for the familiar hell-fire integral to demonic vision: the black figure becomes dominated by the "glare of his ceaseless eyeballs in his mud-daubed face as though they were worked from lungs" (122).

The ending of "Red Leaves," in which the Negro is recaptured and goes to his sacrifice, while forcefully depicting the black man's new human stature, also shows the influence of the Southerner's involuntary reflex against black rebellion. The sense of black humanity is felt in the final image of the protagonist as he seems to tower over lesser characters: "The Negro was the tallest there, his high, close, mud-caked head looming above them all" (129). The description gives an almost biblical significance to the idea of walking tall: he "walked among them, taller than any" (130). The rudiments of demonic vision associated with black di.sorder persist, however, and the conclusion suggests the familiar impulse to repress the Negro. The sense of containing the black man's threat occurs in a final double reference to the protagonist's eyes, which still emit a surreal light, but now are effectively controlled: they are at last "his wild, restrained, unceasing eyes" (129), casting "a wild, restrained glare" (131).

The existence of this impulse in the conclusion gives another meaning to the direction of the plot, which after all follows a pattern similar to that seen in *Huckleberry Finn*. Here black freedom also is undercut by renewed captivity, and here also upon escaping the black protagonist is bitten by a poisonous snake, made the subject of a suggestively gratuitous punishment, in much the same way as Nigger Jim is on Jackson's Island. There is even a shadow of the corruption which sweeps the ending of *Huckleberry Finn,* as the humanistic considerations of art are compromised by repressive unconscious attitudes. For dominating the end of "Red Leaves" is the result of the cottonmouth's bite, the putrid image of the Negro's arm which first "swelled, and it smelled bad" (127), then withered until "it was no larger than that of a child" (127). The black man has in effect been maimed for his temerity. The shrunken arm seems a final symbol of the involuntary reservation in Faulkner's concept of black humanity.

The expression of the Negro in "Pantaloon in Black" follows a pattern similar to that seen in "Red Leaves." Here, as in the earlier tale, a black protagonist is thrust into a highly unstable situation, in this instance induced by the sudden death of his young wife. The black, Rider, also commits a radical action against the white establishment, not a rebellion against literal indentureship, but the murder of a white who habitually exploits Negroes. And here too, with the crime a human component of internal complexity coalesces in the black's characterization; this story ends with the

Negro's assertion: "Hit look lack Ah just cant quit thinking. Look lack Ah just cant quit.''[25] But this tale is set in the contemporary South; it lacks the historical distance which muted point of view in the earlier work. Immediacy seems to shift the balance in Faulkner's racial attitudes. In this story racial disorder influences the narrative to the extent of clouding the black's characterization with a sense of menace similar to that which lurks within the depiction of Joe Christmas. More than any of Faulkner's works but *Light in August,* "Pantaloon in Black'' illustrates the degree of influence still exerted upon the Southern imagination by demonic racial vision.

Extremes echoing earlier Southern fiction in fact dominate the narrative in "Pantaloon in Black.'' At the very time its black protagonist emerges as a compelling human figure, his description is characterized by the elements of demonic vision. Again the Negro's eyes act as a gauge of his unconscious role. Rider's eyes grow fiery red: at first "the whites of his eyes [are] rimmed with red and with something urgent and strained about them'' (142-43). Then "the whites of his eyes [are] covered a little more by the creeping red'' (144). Finally they are "without vision . . . [and] no white showed at all'' (147). Concurrently, his physical description, from an early start in which height and weight are stressed, becomes symbolic. He seems increasingly insubstantial, in hovering motion, with his giant dog appearing like "two shadows flitting broken and intermittent among the trees'' (142), ghostly, "his striding shadow and the trotting one of the dog travelling swift as those of two clouds along the hill'' (148). His strength too approaches omnipotence. At one point he lifts an immense log, overcoming its "primal inertia'' (145). As this story progresses, its Negro protagonist assumes the capacity to enact demonically primordial disorder.

The black's desperate assertion of individuality, the racial murder, also seems as much surreal as real. Nilon describes Rider's use of the weapon, his razor, in which "not even the first jet of blood touched his hand or arm'' (154), as a "perfect act'' displaying "a perfection not found among lesser men.''[26] Certainly the old supernatural associations of black danger are apparent here, and they bring Faulkner's ambivalence toward his protagonist to a crisis. That a defensive reaction repressing the black figure was inevitable had become evident in Rider's persistent cry, which echoed the fate of earlier threatening Negroes, "Ah'm snakebit and bound to die" (152). But the degree to which the narrative is influenced could hardly be anticipated. At the point that the protagonist enacts his surreal violence, the moment at which his black humanity flourishes, he is simply purged from the narrative in a way similar to that seen in much earlier Southern fiction.

In a transformation as jarring as any found in the *Sut Lovingood Yarns* which Faulkner so much admired, the entire setting, narrative voice, and tone of the story shift to an expression of total social stability. The scene becomes that of a white kitchen in which a "wife was cooking supper" (154). The point of view is that of her husband, "the sheriff's deputy who had been officially in charge of the business" (154). Rider already has been lynched, and his surreal disorder has become the buffoonery of "them damn niggers," inexplicable "because they aint human" (154). It is the telling through such a bemused, condenscending voice that efficiently disarms surely the most threatening of all Rider's surreal acts, his omnipotent transcendence of physical barriers: the deputy relates watching the protagonist in jail as he "comes and grabs holt of that steel barred door and rips it out of the wall, bricks hinges and all, and walks out of the cell toting the door over his head like it was a gauze window-screen" (158). The narrative technique finally lays to rest the vision of Rider's superhuman capacities by transforming them into the comic hyperbole characteristic of Southwestern humor. In the deputy's point of view Rider lies trapped, "laughing, with tears big as glass marbles running across his face and down past his ears and making a kind of popping sound on the floor like somebody dropping bird eggs, laughing and laughing" (159). The final point of the story confirms a return to normality with a vision of white womanhood setting out alone into the restored safety of a Southern night, "going to the picture show" (159). In a manner not dissimilar to that seen in *Tom*

Sawyer, a minor celebration confirms the successful purgation from this narrative of racial danger.

An awareness of the influence upon Faulkner of such traditional Southern attitudes explains an unrecognized contradiction in the racial vision of his most complex attempt to understand the meaning of blackness, *Light in August* (1932). The approach to racial problems in this work appears definitively analytic; as Olga Vickery points out, the protagonist Joe Christmas "has a dual function in the novel. As an individual, he explores his own relation to the myth of the Negro, while as a part of society, he is identified with the myth."[27] In form, as Richard Chase claims, it resembles the naturalistic novel: "There are heredity, environment, neurotic causation, social maladjustment. What happens later to Joe Christmas is made inevitable by the circumstances of his boyhood."[28] The nature of such influences is hinted at by Kazin, who suggests that the protagonist "is an abstraction created by the racist mania of his grandfather, a former preacher whose tormented life is spent insisting that Negroes are guilty in the eyes of God."[29] Yet Kazin just scratches the surface of the role of black damnation in *Light in August*. Old Doc Hines is not the only character equating blackness with diabolism in the novel. The birth, initiation, and death of the protagonist are all determined by similar figures. And alone in the novel, each of these fundamentally influential characters display god-like powers; they are invested with the surreal capabilities traditionally associated with demonic vision. In thought this novel may seem analytic, in form naturalistic; but in each of these fundamental respects the very conception of *Light in August* is warped by the irrationality associated with its demonic vision.

The diabolical vision of Christmas's grandfather, Hines, is not only the first, but the most clearly defined racial point of view that the protagonist encounters. There is no mistaking the nature of Hines's beliefs; for him Christmas is "the devil's laidby crop,"[30] "he was the one that laid it by" (358). His crucial role as the "instrument" (360) by which to "put the mark, . . . to put the knowledge" (351) of racial damnation upon the young protagonist involves gaining a literal control over the infant, a nearly impossible matter of a midnight pursuit of his runaway daughter and her dark-skinned seducer. Hines sets out on the chase with the full confidence that it would be "the devil that guided him" (355). And he is guided; if it is not "the devil . . . [who] showed [him] the right road and . . . held the pistol steady" (356), some supernatural agency performs the task. For against all reason, Hines finds the couple:

> He could not have known . . . where the gal was then. . . . [But he] took the only short cut he could possibly have taken, choosing it in the dark, out of a half dozen of them, that would ever have caught up with them. And yet it wasn't any possible way that he could have known which road they had taken. But he did. He found them like he had known all the time just where they would be. . . . It was like he knew. It was pitch dark, and even when he caught up with a buggy, there wasn't any way he could have told it was the one he wanted. (355)

This logically inexplicable situation occurs once again at the second crucial juncture in Christmas's development, accounting for the episode which precipitates the protagonist into his adult wanderings on "the street which was to run for fifteen years" (210). It also involves a character obsessed with damnation, McEachern, the foster father in whose home Christmas reached adolescence. McEachern, discovering Christmas at a dance, draws the same association of the protagonist with the devil: he "struck at the face of the youth . . . and perhaps when the face ducked the blow and came up again it was not the face of that child. . . . It was the face of Satan, which he knew as well" (191). This pivotal figure too seeks out the dance at which he falls victim to his foster son's violence through the same surreal agency as that which motivated Hines: he searches with "both omnipotence and clairvoyance. . . . [He rides] straight to the place which he sought and which he had found out of a whole night and almost a whole half of a county. . . . He had had neither reason nor manner of knowing that there would be a dance held in it" (190).

With the third and final of these episodes, involving Percy
Grimm's execution of Christmas, a quality suggesting endorsement comes to characterize the surrealistic opposition to black
diabolism. Grimm too equates blackness with damnation,
exclaiming as he castrates the protagonist, "Now you'll let white
women alone, even in hell!" (439). He too moves against Christmas during the abortive escape attempt with "certitude, the blind
and untroubled faith in the rightness and infallibility of his
actions" (434). But no longer does such power seem to be the odd
and inexplicable result of insanity, as with the "violently fanatical
and a little crazed" (322) Hines, or the "furious and dreamlike"
(191) McEachern. Now it seems almost conventional, the expression of the established supernatural power at work in man's affairs.
Grimm acts "with the delicate swiftness of an apparition, the
implacable undeviation of Juggernaut or Fate" (435); "as though
under the protection of a magic or a providence" (437); "with that
lean, swift, blind obedience to whatever Player moved him on the
Board" (437). Indeed, repressing the momentarily "free" black
disorder, Grimm's supernatural powers take on the positive overtones of a religious sanctification. His face displaying "that
serene, unearthly luminousness of angels in church windows"
(437), "his young voice clear and outraged like that of a young
priest" (439), leading vigilantes who seem radiant "as though
from haloes" (438), Grimm appears a figure of transcendent
salvation.

There is a narrative logic about the transcendence of repressive
impulses in Percy Grimm. By the time of his pursuit, Christmas
has emerged as a fully realized expression of demonic vision. The
fulfillment of the early surreal influences of Hines and McEachern
upon the protagonist is complex, for the crystallization of the
diabolic point of view apparently requires Christmas's total
acquiescence to the social idea of his blackness which follows the
murder of Joanna Burden. To be racially demonic he must first
completely act like a Negro. He is drawn into this self-vision by the
white reaction to his crime, which, while it has served as an
expression of individualism, has also stirred the threat of racial

disorder. The consequent irrationality, sweeping aside all doubts of Christmas's blackness, forces the protagonist, as Vickery points out, "to exemplify [the category of blackness] in the sequence of flight and pursuit, capture and death. . . . As Christmas recognizes the inevitability of this pattern and of his own part in it, he visualizes himself sinking 'at last into the black abyss.' "[31]

This process, which elaborates upon the pattern discussed in the two stories, is anticipated in an unrecognized manner earlier in Christmas's development. For Joanna Burden may not be Christmas's first murder victim. Through his attack upon McEachern the protagonist also moved to define himself through violence against conventional morality, attempting to "put behind now at once and for all the Shalt Not, [to be] free at last of honor and law" (194). This crime too in an oblique way produces punishment in the form of a savage beating at the hands of disreputable whites. It also evokes the first explicit question about Christmas's blackness. Ominously, a white stranger appears at that moment to demand: *"Is he really a nigger? He dont look like one"* (205). The answer anticipates the eipsode depicting Grimm's conclusive repression of Christmas: *"We'll find out. We'll see if his blood is black. . . . We'll need a little more blood to tell for sure"* (205). Tellingly, at this point the narrative gives imagistic indication that through racial crime Christmas has embarked toward the full emergence of his blackness. At this pivotal point in his life the tentative white outlines of the protagonist's portrayal seem to fade to blackness "like a picture in chalk being erased from a blackboard" (195).

At this moment the first suggestions of the surreal capacities in Christmas's depiction which ultimately will allow him against all physiological reason to sever Joanna Burden's neck bone begin to surface. Upon felling McEachern, Christmas suddenly acts as if he has had omniscience communicated to him: "He could not have known where McEachern had left the horse, nor for certain if it was even there. Yet he ran straight to it, with something of his adopted father's complete faith in an infallibility in events" (193-94). For an instant in this state Christmas seems a diabolical dark

figure; damned, "as Faustus" (194); Satanic, "his teeth shining
in the lamp" (195); about him swirling a hint of hell-fire, "sul-
phuric; the invisible wind flew past" (194).

Such demonic characteristics seem finally to explode into
expression at the point when the protagonist, a confessed racial
killer ready to "plead guilty and take a life sentence" (433),
irrationally escapes and in regard to the white imagination
becomes a symbol of unrestrained black disorder. The brief
episode is a microcosmic depiction of demonic vision, its imagery
as hyperbolic as that seen in some of the *Sut Lovingood Yarns.*
The entire setting pulsates with an almost tangible sense of threat;
in response to the danger the fire alarm is set off: "At that moment
the fire siren sounded for the first time, beginning and mounting to
a slow and sustained scream that seemed at last to pass beyond the
realm of hearing, into that of sense, like soundless vibration"
(435). In this telescoped episode Christmas initially seems minis-
cule, remote, the characteristic flashes of fire brief and almost
harmless: "Then he saw Christmas. He saw the man, small with
distance, appear up out of the ditch, his hands close together. As
Grimm watched he saw the fugitive's hands glint once like the
flash of a heliograph as the sun struck the handcuffs. . . . Then the
tiny figure ran again and vanished beyond the nearest negro cabin"
(436). But he grows with surreal swiftness, "with an effect as of
magic" (436). Appearing again, he carries "a heavy nickel-plated
pistol" (437) inexplicably acquired, which immeasurably intensifies his danger. Now his fiery presence looms, the "manacled
hands high and now glinting as if they were on fire" (436).

In this fantastic state, a flaming supernatural figure with "raised
and armed and manacled hands full of glare and glitter like lightning bolts, so that he resembled a vengeful and furious god
pronouncing a doom" (438), Christmas is finally eliminated from
the narrative. In the very act of his purgation, the irrational cause
for the narrative's repressive stance toward the protagonist seems
confirmed. During this definitive response to Christmas's second
racial crime, the question asked after his first is answered. Finally
the "little more" blood necessary to ascertain the protagonist's

racial nature is obtained, and it indeed seems black: "From out the slashed garments about his hips and loins the pent black blood seemed to rush like a released breath" (440). It is this basic metaphor of blackness, black blood, upon which is focused the full impact of the narrative's demonic vision. For while, as Vickery points out, at this moment of death Christmas finally transcends the external classification of "Negro," simultaneously the narrative gives its most basic expression of the character's subjective demonic component. What seems almost a religious depiction of the very spirit of "the man" seems distorted by the traditional fiery imagery of demonic vision: his black blood "seemed to rush out of his pale body like the rush of sparks from a rising rocket; . . . [a] black blast" (440). In Faulkner's narrative, even at the last, the expression of the black man displays the surreal influence of demonic vision.

In a manner more telling than that seen in *Huckleberry Finn,* the results of the Southern artist's ambivalence find expression in *Light in August*. In the earlier book as art is turned to the uses of repression a sense of malaise grows in the narrative, leading ultimately to the diseased transformations which characterize the very language spoken at the Phelps's slave-holding plantation. In *Light in August,* as racial attitudes in the environment darken, a similar situation occurs. But in this novel the full consequences are focused upon a single character, Gail Hightower.

Kazin recognizes the centrality of Hightower's role in suggesting that he is "both a surrogate figure for Faulkner's meditations and a kind of scapegoat on whom Faulkner can discharge his exasperation with Southern nostalgia."[32] Yet Hightower's relationship with the author goes still further. He is an artist of sorts himself, a painter, a photographer, an art instructor. He is first known by "his monument," "the sign . . . he painted" (52) to advertise his skills. Itself a work of art, it reads in "bits of broken glass contrived cunningly into the paint, . . . the letters glittered with an effect as of Christmas: Rev. Gail Hightower, D.D./Art Lessons/Handpainted Xmas & Anniversary Cards/Photographs Developed" (53). As well as a philosophical vehicle, Hightower serves as the reflection within the narrative of a crucial aspect of the author's artistic personality.

Hightower depicts the Southern artist in his most aesthetically destructive situation. This function can be seen in the sense of danger which hovers about him all out of proportion to his flaccid passivity. He contains a quantity ugly and threatening, his "flabby and obese stomach like some monstrous pregnancy" (291); it is "as if there were something in his flabby paunch fatal and highly keyed, like dynamite" (381). He carries dehumanizing racial views, attitudes that starkly resemble those seen in the antebellum fiction of John Pendleton Kennedy and William Gilmore Simms. One of the three "phantoms" which dominate his life is an old black woman, freed in 1865, who in a manner similar to the earlier stereotyped darkies questions freedom: " 'Free?' she said. She spoke with still and brooding scorn. 'Free? Whut's freedom done except git Marse Gail killed and made a bigger fool outen Pawmp den even de Lawd Hisself could do? Free? Dont talk ter me erbout freedom' " (451-52). But grimmer racial attitudes account for the danger associated with this figure. Underlying the very essence of his aesthetic capabilities, the flashing "Christmas" effect of his sign, the "Xmas" pictures he paints, his photographic developing, is a shadowy yet fundamental relationship with the ultimately diabolical figure who himself at a crucial point appears "out of the darkness like a kodak print emerging from the liquid" (100), Joe Christmas. Blurred and muted, Hightower's artistic potential is symbolically associated with the development of the narrative's demonic protagonist. Surely the aspect of the author Hightower expresses is encapsulated in the photograph taken of him fleeing his church, his face hidden by a hymnal. In the oblique, ruthlessly prying image of the camera this face of the artist behind the book is momentarily, astonishingly diabolical: "Behind the book his lips were drawn back as though he were smiling. But his teeth were tight together and his face looked like the face of Satan in the old prints" (63).

A scapegoat not merely for Faulkner's disgust at Southern nostalgia but for the author's sense of helplessness at being entrapped in an antihumanistic Southern tradition, Hightower seems a hopeless figure in the narrative. It is difficult to see how Hightower's final epiphany, which occurs apparently while dying, in regard to racial attitudes in *Light in August* serves as anything other than a statement of irresolution. Hightower, who with one ineffectual exception rejects any responsibility to Christmas, experiences a definitive vision of all the narrative's characters, and among them only the protagonist remains unresolved, vibrating between self-realization and ruthless repression, his face ceaselessly shifting from his own to that of Percy Grimm:

> This face alone is not clear. It is confused more than any other, as though in the now peaceful throes of a more recent, a more inextricable, compositeness. Then he can see that it is two faces which seem to strive (but not of themselves striving or desiring it . . .) in turn to free themselves one from the other, then fade and blend again. But he has seen now, the other face, the one that is not Christmas. "Why, it's . . ." he thinks. "I have seen it, recently . . . Why, it's that . . . boy. With that black pistol, automatic they call them. The one who . . . into the kitchen where . . . killed, who fired the . . ." Then it seems to him that some ultimate dammed flood within him breaks and rushes away." (465; except for the first, the ellipses are Faulkner's)

This image of the artist seems to enlarge the meaning of corruption, his face "slick, as if it had been oiled" (370), with "rotting teeth from about which the long sagging of flabby and putty-colored flesh falls away" (370). Wounded by the dark diabolical figure with whose creation he is strangely involved, his "bandaged head huge and without depth upon the twin blobs of his hands" (467), this maimed figure is a paradigm of the anguish of the Southern artist.

Conclusion

Recent American Writings:
The Leveling of Racial Vision

In the years around and after World War Two, the drift in the bulk of Southern writings toward realistic or self-conciously symbolic uses of racial material became virtually conclusive. A firm analytic tone came to define a great part of the fiction about the Negro. As Louise Y. Gossett makes clear, many Southern writers such as Erskine Caldwell treat blacks in a realistic sociological context, sometimes exploiting them "for the sake of social or economic theories."[1] The sense of reassessment common to the postwar view of the Negro is encapsulated in a discussion which occurs early in Elizabeth Spencer's *The Voice at the Back Door,* involving the diplomacy of a black mistress attending the funeral of her white Southern sheriff lover. *"Couldn't* she go?'' a character asks. " 'I don't know,' [another] answered thoughtfully. 'Before the war, I could have said for sure, I think, that she would take a big risk to go. Since the war, I don't know.' ''[2] The subjective writings are no less deliberate in the treatment of the black man. Authors such as Eudora Welty and Flannery O'Connor have compared themselves, or been compared, to Nathaniel Hawthorne in their uses of racial symbolism.[3] Because of these developments, paralleling the "two important changes" which Frederick J. Hoffman finds "have occurred in more recent examples of Southern literature: the shifting of scene from the land to the city, and the intellectual and moral change, from the Southern past to the contemporary universal,"[4] the distinctions between Southern and Northern expressions of the Negro have blurred.

With the rarest exceptions, contemporary Southern fiction reflects the levelings of nationalization in its depictions of the black man.

II

What few examples of the old spontaneous expression of racial disorder that do occur in recent Southern fiction seem more than anything else to be anachronisms, curious echoes of a past fictional mode. The episode in Thomas Wolfe's *The Web and the Rock* involving the black Dick Prosser's murderous rampage demonstrates the situation. As Paschal Reeves points out, Wolfe's "presentation of the Negro in [this episode] is in keeping with the traditional Southern attitude."[5] Accordingly, the description of the black's murder of several white townspeople incorporates a great deal of the traditional demonic imagery. The racial violence awakens a fiery glow in Nebraska Crane, an Indian: "Nebraska's coal black eyes were shining now with a savage sparkle even they had never had before. The awakened blood of the Cherokee was smoking in him."[6] The air is filled with the sounds of danger: "They heard behind them, at the edge of Niggertown, coming towards them now, growing, swelling at every instant, one of the most savagely mournful and terrifying sounds that night can know. It was the baying of the hounds as they came up upon the leash from Niggertown. Full-throated, howling deep, the savagery of blood was in it, and the savagery of man's guilty doom was in it, too" (143-44). After the Negro's execution, the episode provokes the following reflection from the narrator:

> [The Negro] came from darkness. He came out of the heart of darkness, from the dark heart of the secret and undiscovered South. . . . He was night's child and partner, a token of the wonder and the mystery, the other side of man's dark soul, his nighttime partner, and his nighttime foal, a symbol of those things that pass by darkness and that still remain, of something still and waiting in the night that comes and passes and that will abide, a symbol of man's

evil innocence, and the token of his mystery, a projection of his own unfathomed quality, a friend, a brother, and a mortal enemy, an unknown demon. (156)

Yet, in a manner sharply differing from earlier expressions of racial disorder, in this modern narrative in spite of the demonic images of devilish fire, of danger, the "savagery of man's guilty doom," of the nightmarishness of "an unknown demon," no further repercussions are felt. As Gossett points out, "It is significant that Wolfe treats the incident as impersonal and self-contained."[7] While a shadow of the old psychological impulse remains, time and an uncongenially analytical environment have conspired to divorce the demonic racial expression from its sources of unconscious power. As in the above passage, the subjective basis becomes explicit, and denied its essential spontaneity, demonic vision no longer carries its former narrative influence.

A similar situation occurs in Carson McCullers's *The Heart is a Lonely Hunter*. As Ihab Hassan suggests, McCullers's work in the same way as more recent Southern fiction is universal in its concerns and largely sociological in its treatment of the black man: "Through [the Negro Doctor Benedict] Copeland and Blount, the novel gains its force of social reference; the idea of fascism abroad is constantly played off against that of racism at home."[8] As in Wolfe's novel, elements of the old demonic imagery are evoked by the vision of racial disorder—in this case the eruptions of Doctor Copeland's frustrations—"a black, terrible, Negro feeling."[9] "The hopeless suffering of his people made in him a madness, a wild and evil feeling of destruction. At times he drank strong liquor and beat his head against the floor. In his heart there was a savage violence" (111). But when Copeland feels "as though he had swelled up to the size of a giant . . . his chest a dynamo, . . . [and would] call out in a giant voice" (149), the narrative suddenly offers a curious internal vision of its central black man. Copeland opens his own medical history: "In the folder were several lung X-rays and a short case history. He held an X-ray up to the light. On the upper left lung there was a bright place like a calcified star. . . . At the finish there were three words: 'Prognosis: Don't know' " (151). In this photograph the mechanics of the "dynamo" in the Negro's chest are laid bare. The once flashing images of light associated with demonic energy have atrophied; within Copeland there is "a calcified star." It is an indication not of power, but of disease. It is as if this photograph, plumbing to the soul of the black man in a way that extends the meaning of the photographic metaphor of dissolution seen in the case of William Faulkner's Joe Christmas, indicates by its very form the doubtful "Prognosis" of the dying demonic tradition.

Such enervation at the core of spontaneous racial expression may help explain a curious ambiguity in the narrative of Flannery O'Connor's novel, *Wise Blood*. The central action in this tortured novel is the theft, in accordance with the promptings of his "wise blood," by a zoo guard named Enoch Emery of a shrunken museum mummy. The mummy is given as a gift to Hazel Motes, a character in search of a new set of purified religious values. Most readers find that, as Martha Stephens puts it, "the Enoch Emery parable . . . is meant to operate as a kind of parody of the religious search of Hazel Motes"; in Preston M. Browning, Jr.'s words, that the mummy is a symbol "representing secular society's corruption and fraudulence."[10] But if such a simple opposition exists in the narrative, it is hard to account for the hesitation surrounding the Enoch Emery story. As Stephens points out:

> It has been disconcerting for many readers that the stories of Hazel and Enoch do not really converge, on the narrative level, after the tussle outside the museum (that Hazel is never even aware, as far as we know, that Sabbath's "baby" is Enoch's new jesus, the museum mummy); that Enoch simply drops out of the book dressed up in a gorilla suit himself and terrorizing a courting couple on a hillside overlooking the city; that, in other words, we never get the final revelation about this character that the novel has seemed to be leading us to.[11]

It is hardly adequate to attribute this narrative problem to O'Connor's difficulty in handling the complexities of the novel format; *Wise Blood* is not exactly mammoth in its dimensions.[12] Rather it is likely that the central symbol of the mummy was destined to carry a darker and more intense function than that of parody, and that somehow it proved deficient in content. In the case of *Wise Blood,* for one of the first times the Southern imagination of primordial evil has proved inadequate.

In *Wise Blood,* the image of the mummy seems intended to stand for nothing less than the anti-Christ; as Kathleen Feeley puts it, "The origin of Enoch's wise blood seems diabolical; it is a negative counterpart of the blood of Redemption."[13] As such it is the product of a "creative process" in which John Hawkes finds "the writer's objective Catholic knowledge of the devil [is transformed] into an authorial attitude in itself in some measure diabolical."[14] In the search for an image of sufficient dark power to convey the sense of Satanic evil it is almost inevitable that after a century of demonic expression racial material would percolate into the author's imagination. Surely this particularly Southern relationship accounts for the final objectification of Emery's evil instincts; the nighttime scene in which the white boy dons his stolen gorilla's costume is fraught with racial connotations. In it Emery is transformed into a black bestial form: "In the uncertain light, one of his lean white legs could be seen to disappear and then the other, one arm and then the other: a black heavier shaggier figure replaced his. For an instant, it had two heads, one light and one dark, but after a second, it pulled the dark black head over the other and corrected this."[15] Surely it also accounts for the veritable catalog of imagery characteristic of past demonic narratives: much as in Tom Driscoll's murder scene in Mark Twain's *Pudd'nhead Wilson,* Emery steals the mummy from the museum after "he had darkened his face and hands with brown shoe polish" (174). Carrying the figure, he appears strikingly like the Swamp Doctor in Henry Clay Lewis's tale, "Stealing a Baby": "He was carrying something about the size of a baby, wrapped up in newspapers" (173). The journey to Hazel Motes's rooms with the figure is as surrealistic as any in *Light in August:* "He had never been to

Hazel Motes's place before but the instinct that was guiding him was very sure of itself'' (174). When the mummy is finally described through Emery's point of view, the image reverberates with past demonic phraseology: it is "a dead shriveled-up part-nigger dwarf'' (176). In its very echo of the diabolical racial association, O'Connor's novel demonstrates the exhaustion of the demonic tradition in the case of the Negro in a manner similar to that seen with the Indian in Faulkner's "Red Leaves,'' a story in which red men also appear in the form of museum artifacts. As the critical confusion suggests, an endorsement of neither heaven nor hell can result from the evocation of the flaccid subjective connotations of this atrophied black relic.

III

Just how far removed *Wise Blood* is from the previous eruptions of demonic expression can be judged by the use of the Negro in O'Connor's other major piece of racial fiction, "The Artificial Nigger.'' This story recounts a journey to the city by a boy and his grandfather, in which the grandson is to be exposed to a full experiential reality: "He's never seen anything before,'' the grandfather confides, he is "ignorant as the day he was born, but I mean for him to get his fill once and for all.'' "[I] don't hold nothing back.''[16] Both the old man and the boy are callow; they are rivals of a sort, and continually at odds. Lost in the city, they encounter at last a statue of a Negro: "It was not possible to tell if the artificial Negro were meant to be young or old; he looked too miserable to be either. He was meant to look happy because his mouth was stretched up at the corners but the chipped eye and the angle he was cocked at gave him a wild look of misery instead'' (127). Facing it, the two whites experience an epiphany, and are reconciled: "Mr. Head looked like an ancient child and Nelson like a miniature old man. They stood gazing at the artificial Negro as if they were faced with some great mystery, some monument to another's victory that brought them together in their common defeat. They could both feel it dissolving their differences like an action of mercy" (127-28). Both return home the better for their experience, redeemed: "He saw that no sin was too monstrous for him to claim as his own, and since God loved in proportion as He forgave, he felt ready at that instant to enter Paradise" (129).

The differences in the structure of this narrative compared to that of previous evocations of subjective racial associations are immediately apparent. As Gilbert Muller has demonstrated, the structure of O'Connor's story resembles the universal archetype of "man's capacity for suffering, damnation, and salvation,"[17] as depicted in Dante's allegory. Whereas in the earlier Southern fiction, expressing the unconscious energy of the black image unstabilized the narrative, in this instance it leads to a resolution and spiritual enlightenment. The central symbol in a universalized allegory of hope, the Negro conveys in this tale an essentially conventional aura of mystery: "It is inscrutable and mysterious, a symbol of universal suffering";[18] "a symbol of that which is beyond the ordinary, that which transcends man's expectations and eludes his calculations, in brief, that which is mysterious."[19] If not exactly benign, in this example of recent racial symbolism the Negro has lost the numinous terror of primordial disorder unique to the earlier Southern fiction.

Such a usage of racial imagery far more resembles the expressions of the black man in writings by Northerners such as Herman Melville and Nathaniel Hawthorne than it does the major part of Southern fiction. Muller draws the parallel between "the equivocal figure of the Negro" in "The Artificial Nigger," and Melville's use of the black man in "Benito Cereno."[20] The similarity between the aura of universal mystery displayed by the black in "The Artificial Nigger" and that associated with the Negro in *Moby-Dick* (1851) is inescapable. In Melville's novel the protagonist is also "mysteriously drawn towards" Queequeg, and finally comes to see the black man as the very objectification of cosmic mystery:

[Queequeg's] tattooing, had been the work of a departed prophet and seer of his island, who, by those hieroglyphic marks, had written out on his body a complete theory of the heavens and the earth, and a mystical treatise on the art of attaining truth; so that Queequeg in his own proper person was a riddle to unfold; a wondrous work in one volume; but whose mysteries not even himself could read, though his own live heart beat against them; and these mysteries were therefore destined in the end to moulder away with the living parchment whereon they were inscribed, and so be unsolved to the last. And this thought it must have been which suggested to Ahab that wild exclamation of his, when one morning turning away from surveying poor Queequeg—''Oh, devilish tantalization of the gods!''[21]

In the Melville passage, as in O'Connor's racial image, the subjective significance of blackness displays the remoteness of a theoretical metaphysic.

Perhaps the universalization—or at least the deregionalization—of the racial image in recent Southern fiction is most apparent in exploring what O'Connor has called her ''kinship with Hawthorne,'' which she feels is more powerful ''than with any other American writer.''[22] When O'Connor depicts the mystery of blackness, she writes as much out of her awareness of the allegorical pattern for the expression of the surreal established by the Northern author as she does in response to her own Southern intuitions. The similarities between the structure of ''The Artificial Nigger'' and Hawthorne's ''My Kinsman, Major Molineux'' are too apparent to dwell on. In each story, prompted by the encounter with a racial image of mystery—in the case of Hawthorne's tale it is a figure ''one side of [whose] face blazed an intense red, while the other was black as midnight''[23]—a young protagonist matures, coming to understand the ''overwhelming humiliation'' of an older relative, in Hawthorne's narrative the deposed colonial governor.

The relationship between O'Connor's story and Hawthorne's allegory, *The Blithedale Romance* (1852), is more subtle, but no less fundamental. The sequence of encounters with Negroes is initiated by a striking image in O'Connor's story:

A huge coffee-colored man was coming slowly forward. He had on a light suit and a yellow satin tie with a ruby pin in it. One of his hands rested on his stomach which rode majestically under his buttoned coat, and in the other he held the head of a black walking stick that he picked up and set down with a deliberate outward motion each time he took a step. He was proceeding very slowly. . . . The light from a sapphire ring on the brown hand that picked up the cane reflected in Mr. Head's eye. (109-10)

In *The Blithedale Romance,* the surreal figure of mysterious power, Westervelt, displays "the effect of an apparition." He is "well and fashionably dressed. . . . There was a gold chain, exquisitely wrought, across his vest. I never saw a smoother or whiter gloss than that upon his shirt-bosom, which had a pin in it, set with a gem that glimmered . . . like a living tip of fire. He carried a stick with a wooden head, carved in vivid imitation of that of a serpent."[24] Beyond such overt borrowings as the emphasis upon walking sticks and brilliant gems, the similarity in tone between the two passages suggests the degree to which O'Connor's racial imagery is indebted to a form of allegory essentially alien to the temper of Southern fiction.

Other expressions of this widespread recent development in the usage of black symbolism in Southern fiction occur in writings by Shirley Ann Grau and William Styron. Grau's story, "The Black Prince" appears at first glance a throwback to the earlier racial fiction, since, as Gossett points out, its "protagonist is Stanley Albert, a fine black incarnation of Lucifer. . . . [He is an] agent of evil."[25] Materializing out of nothing, "out of the morning fog,"[26] "out of a patch of bright moon ground, where there were only brown pine needles" (61), this Satanic Negro wreaks havoc among the population of a small black Southern town. He seems devilish enough; when he helps fight a fire "the water was like kerosene in his hands. Wherever he'd toss a bucketful, the fire would shoot up, brighter and hotter than before" (57). Yet in this bit of white fiction, every action is distanced by the exclusion of any suggestion of an influence upon the white world by all the violence. In the isolated homogeneously black environment, the disorder is the Negro's problem. Moreover, whatever subjective impact remains is undercut by the sense that the piece is a deliberate rendering of folklore elements into an arbitrarily black format. There seems little to be gained by having it black men who comment upon the ugliness of this devil's shadow, and cast the silver bullets by which he is exorcised, except possibly to suggest that Negroes too can be seduced by the devil's ability to coin money out of thin air. Rather than conveying any of the old spontaneity, this self-conscious tale only serves, in Gossett's words, as a parable of the "hedonist" and "Puritan" Southern responses to "pleasure, leisure, luxury, and wealth."[27]

A similarly explicit symbolic use is made of Negro religion in William Styron's *Lie Down in Darkness*. The grimness of Styron's novel is to an extent redeemed by its conclusion, in which a black religious festival is described. The image of "de prime sanctua'y, de alpha and de omega, where all mysteries are revealed,"[28] underscores Gossett's comment that in this novel "only the Negroes . . . have the capacity to love and to believe":[29]

> [The raft] lay anchored offshore in the shallow water, bobbing gently in the waves. On it had been erected a sort of stage, surrounded on four sides by a golden damask curtain; embroidered designs—dragons and crosses and crowns, Masonic emblems, shields, bizarre and unheard-of animals, an amalgam of myth and pagan ritual and Christian symbology—all these glowed against the curtain in green and red phosphorescent fabrics, literally hurting the eyes. At the corners of the curtain were tall golden rods, and surmounting each was a transparent globe, through which an electric bulb shone, giving outline to painted red letters, which said simply: LOVE. (392)

But it is perhaps the stories of Eudora Welty which most tellingly illustrate the overt uses made of racial symbolism in recent Southern fiction. "A Worn Path" and "Powerhouse" center upon Negroes who display what has become the usual black mystical oneness with nature, or the embodiment of cosmic perception.

Phoenix Jackson, the ancient black woman journeying through woods in "A Worn Path," is intimately associated with the "foxes, owls, beetles, jack rabbits, coons and wild animals"[30] of the forest. Indeed, she herself seems to have blended into the natural world: "Her skin had a pattern all its own of numberless branching wrinkles . . . as though a whole little tree stood in the middle of her forehead" (276). Powerhouse, the black jazz musician, "encompassed," in Ruth M. Vande Kieft's words, "all intuitively . . . an unbelievably wide range of knowledge and experience—much of it savage, terrorizing, much of it tender, most of it closed to white people, except insofar as he conveys it through his music."[31] A source of cosmic awareness, he himself is seen in an image suggesting the recent universalization of the black figure: "You can't tell what he is. 'Nigger man?'—he looks more Asiatic, monkey, Jewish, Babylonian, Peruvian, fanatic, devil" (254). The description of his effects upon white listeners seems sharply contemporary in its usage of concepts such as oblivion and void. Welty's use of the black musician to evoke the sense of "oblivion" (255), the lostness at the center of "a whirlpool" (257), the plunge at the edge of "a cliff" (257), all lend substance to Eunice Glenn's remark that while normally resembling Hawthorne, Welty in this story "comes nearer being a twin of Melville."[32]

A contradiction apparent in Welty's "Keela, the Outcast Indian Maiden," may serve to conclude this discussion of the effects upon Southern racial expression of the contemporary ambience. The story itself is a document of reason. It describes the blindness underlying racial prejudice through the association of a white circus barker with a dwarfed, clubfooted Negro whom the circus abducts, paints red, disguises as an Indian woman, and forces to eat chickens alive as a sideshow attraction. The figure seems the very vision of savage bestiality: "If anybody was to even come near it or even bresh their shoulder against the rope it'd growl and take on and shake its iron rod. When it would eat the live chickens it'd growl somethin' awful" (77). The barker contributes to the illusion: through his megaphone he warns that no one approach the figure or "she will only beat your brains out with her iron rod, and eat them alive!" (80). Someone understands the Negro's predicament, and helps—"you know—when that man laid out his open hand on the boards, why, it just let go the iron bar . . . [and] drug itself over to where the fella was standin' an' leaned down an' grabbed holt onto that white man's hand as tight as it could an' cried like a baby. It didn't want to hit him!" (82)—and the barker is devastated by the sudden realization of his own imperceptiveness. Clearly enough the point is that racism destroys the white: "By that time I felt bad. Been feelin' bad ever since. Can't hold onto a job or stay in one place for nothin' in the world" (83). Yet, as Gossett points out, in this seemingly most objective of racial tales, "The Negro is strangely remote and inaccessible."[33] In fact, with his child's shoe and his simple grin, the Negro seems almost to fade from existence in the face of the white's intensity. It is as if, caught in the imperative need of the white author to express the absurdity of racism, the description of the Negro simply submerges in the narrative's prevailing rage for understanding.

IV

The degree of interchangeability between the recent symbolic use of the racial image in the South and the North's prevalent racial expression can be seen by glancing at four representative novels by nonSouthern authors that have recently dominated the national literary scene. In John Updike's *Rabbit Redux,* Norman Mailer's *An American Dream,* Thomas Pynchon's *Gravity's Rainbow,* and Ken Kesey's *One Flew Over the Cuckoo's Nest,* the function of the Negro and the Indian suggests a revitalization for the white community not substantially different from that seen in Southern stories such as O'Connor's "The Artificial Nigger." Whatever differences that are apparent involve matters of degree, not substance. For a bit freer from the racial inhibitions residual in the South, Northern authors may simply undertake more elaborate and extensive discussions of the anatomy of the Negro's and Indian's subjective significance for the white world than do their Southern counterparts.

In John Updike's *Rabbit Redux* the Negro fugitive Skeeter serves to break down the conventional social prejudices—racial, political ones involving the Vietnamese war, sexual—which had been stifling the white protagonist, Rabbit. As Joyce B. Markle points out, "Skeeter in various ways energizes and vitalizes his surroundings"; he "functions as a kind of redeemer figure."[34] As the agent who leads the white to a new life, the black's function is unmistakable. He is given a sort of historical authenticity through the insertion in the narrative of long passages from *The Life and Times of Frederick Douglass,* which document the liberating rage of the Negro. But primarily the role of the black man, to lead America to a rebirth, is emphasized by the repeated usage of marine images which associate the Negro with new life in its most primordial awakenings. Again and again, Skeeter is described in images of this sort of self-conscious primitivism. The initial meeting with Skeeter takes place in a bar in the black section of town. Against an ambience of black singing which "opens up, grows enormous, frightens Rabbit with its enormous black maw of truth," [35] "the place is deep and more complicated than it appears from the outside"; it displays a "marine underglow" (115). At first Skeeter himself suggests primordial ooze, "the backyard cesspool. . . . This black man opens up under him in the same way: a pit of scummed stench impossible to see to the bottom of" (208). Soon the black loses the taint which comes from fear and seems "a chrysalis of mud," "a black crab" (257). Finally, in the scene which verges upon homosexuality, in his nakedness the black man appears "long as an eel, feeding" (283), and for Rabbit the world seems for a moment to turn fluid, with Jill, his mistress, "a mermaid gesturing beneath the skin of the water [and he] floating rigid to keep himself from sinking in terror" (284). And while the fear in the image suggests—and the last words of the book: "He. She. Sleeps. O.K.?" (407) confirms—there are limits to the white's rebirth, the black's regenerative function nevertheless has been effective enough to provide this racial statement with its underlying structure.

Displaying a kind of upbeat intensity, Norman Mailer's use of the black Shago Martin in *An American Dream* is similar to that of Skeeter in Updike's novel. The subjective power that Shago conveys is described through the familiar recent image of jazz music:

> He did not make me think, as other singers often did, of landscapes in Jamaica, of mangoes, honey, and a breast beneath a moon, of tropical love and candy which went from dark to dawn, no, Shago gave you that, he gave you some of that, but there were snakes in his tropical garden, and a wild pig was off in the wilderness with a rip in its flank from the teeth of a puma, he gave you a world of odd wild cries.[36]

The black is like a "dynamo out on the moon" (190), but again the power of the racial image exists primarily for the use of the white. It is transfused into the white narrator, Rojack, in a struggle: "Violence seemed to shake itself free from him each time I smashed him back to the floor and shake itself into me" (193). It builds in Rojack: "I had never had an idea I was this strong" (193). With the "courage, power, and masculinity" derived from the black man, the white is able to overcome the narrative's figure of evil, Barney Kelly, as Barry H. Leeds points out.[37] Interestingly, in this recent work it is the ruthless white industrialist, Kelly, who "is the Devil incarnate."[38] In dividing the narrative's allegiances into those of heaven and hell, the Negro's power for Mailer has been enlisted emphatically on the side of the angels.

In Thomas Pynchon's *Gravity's Rainbow* too black men may display a primordial power: they spring from tribes who worshipped "a powerful symbol of fertility and life," a goddess who, "in touch with Earth's gift for genesis," "feels power flood in through every gate: a river between her thighs, light leaping at the ends of fingers and toes. It is sure and nourishing as sleep. It is a warmth."[39] Transported from Africa to World War Two Germany, where they have learned rocketry and are about to possess a super V-2, these Schwarzkommando seem to offer the renewing alternative to a continuation of the emotional barrenness of white Europeans and Americans, which is encapsulated in the description of an office of Allied war intelligence, "The White Visitation." There:

> the walls read ice. Graffiti of ice the sunless day, glazing the darkening blood brick and terra cotta as if the house is to be preserved weatherless in some skin of clear museum plastic, an architectural document, an old-fashioned apparatus whose use is forgotten. Ice of varying thickness, wavy, blurred, a legend to be deciphered by lords of the winter, Glacists of the region, and argued over in their journals. (72-73)

Yet there is no undue hope about the Negro's role in *Gravity's Rainbow*. For Pynchon's black men are touched by the white psychological process which associates the Negro's color with death:

> Shit, now is the color white folks are afraid of. Shit is the presence of death, not some abstract-arty character with a scythe but the stiff and rotting corpse itself inside the whiteman's warm and private own *asshole,* which is getting pretty intimate. That's what that white toilet's for. You see many brown toilets? Nope, toilet's the color of gravestones, classical columns of mausoleums, that white porcelain's the very emblem of Odorless and Official Death. Shinola shoeshine polish happens to be the color of Shit. Shoeshine boy Malcolm's in the toilet slappin' on the Shinola, working off whiteman's penance on his sin of being born the color of Shit 'n' Shinola. (688)

And these black men, who at one point are hinted to be the objectification of white "repressions . . . [which] *had* incarnated real and living men" (276-77), have assimilated this grimmest of white racial attitudes into their own self-image. "Inside the Schwarzkommando there are forces, at present, who have opted for sterility and death. The struggle is mostly in silence, in the night, in the nauseas and crampings of pregnancies or miscarriages" (316). Projecting in a dramatic manner the split in the white racial vision, Pynchon depicts a crippled and torn black man, his regenerative function left entirely in doubt.

It is fitting to end this study with Ken Kesey's *One Flew Over the Cuckoo's Nest,* for the clarity of this author's social vision results in one of the most balanced of our subjective racial expressions. Like *Gravity's Rainbow,* in a sense Kesey's novel gives a tinge of naiveté to a great deal of other contemporary fiction dealing with race. There is a curious self-centeredness about those works in which, regardless of a past of racial attitudes at best spotted, authors indulge their dream that the reservoir of subjective power associated with the dark American can be turned at will to the most productive of uses. There is none of this illusion in Kesey's work; black men and red show the effects of history in *One Flew Over the Cuckoo's Nest.* They are exhausted, distorted, destroyed. The Negro orderlies are stunted by white cruelty: one is

> a twisted sinewy dwarf the color of cold asphalt. His mother was raped in Georgia while his papa stood by tied to the hot iron stove with plow traces, blood streaming into his shoes. The boy watched from a closet, five years old and squinting his eye to peep out of the crack between the door and the jamb, and he never grew an inch after. Now his eyelids hang loose and thin from his brow.[40]

The Indian narrator, Chief Bromden, is a schizophrenic, committed in a West Coast mental institution, whose family history, in Terence Martin's words, encapsulates the sad "legacy of his people."[41] The virtue of Kesey's novel is that in expressing its impulse to make use of the dark figure in the contemporary manner of redeemer it includes a crucial step missing in most other works. In evoking his surreal Indian giant Kesey finally acknowledges a movement toward atonement in the white racial vision.

It is unnecessary to recapitulate the entire painful process by which the novel's white figure, McMurphy, transfuses the power stemming from centuries of white self-confidence and victory into the Indian, infusing Chief Bromden, as Martin puts it, with "strength, courage, and emerging manhood."[42] When McMurphy arrives in the ward, a transfer from the state farm, the Indian is symbolically shrunken, "sitting there with my knees pulled up and my arms wrapped around them" (22), "quiet as dust" (3). The transformation is anticipated in the moment when McMurphy touches the Indian's hand: "The fingers were thick and strong closing over mine, and my hand commenced to feel peculiar and went to swelling up out there on my stick of an arm, like he was transmitting his own blood into it. It rang with blood and power. It blowed up near as big as his" (24). And its crucial episode is late in the narrative in the electro-therapy room. The place is alive with images of energy. The sounds of "AIR RAID" (271) reverberate through it for the Chief. "Light arcs across" (270), McMurphy is "frosted over completely with sparks" (270). There the final transferal of power from the white to the Indian takes place, for emerging from his shock treatment McMurphy seems like nothing more than a depleted battery, "face frosted white. Corrosion. Battery acid" (271), while for the first time the Chief is strong, whole: "I rubbed my eyes with the heels of my hands and tried to clear my head. I worked at it. I'd never worked at coming out of it before. . . . [I] knew this time I had them beat" (275).

McMurphy fulfills his promise to restore the Indian's strength, to blow him "back up to full size" (211), recreating a dark figure of surrealistic overtones: *"There* you'll be. It's the Big Chief Bromden, cuttin' down the boulevard—men, women, and kids rockin' back on their heels to peer up at him: 'Well well well, what giant's this *here*, takin' ten feet at a step and duckin' for Telephone wires?' " (211). The narrative concludes with a hint that this red man, shaped anew in the proportions of supernatural power with which the white has always seen him and liberated, "taking huge strides as I ran, seeming to step and float a long ways before my next foot struck the earth. . . . Flying. Free" (310), might now succeed in accomplishing the regenerative function all along implicit in his image, finally "baptizing the sleeping earth" (310). Yet if Kesey has wrought the first of American fiction's dark primordial figures untainted by the dissonances of terror, it is, as Martin puts it, "at a cost terribly high and terribly necessary."[43] Making this figure of transcendent freedom and power out of the debris of centuries of hatred and fear has destroyed the white protagonist; after his lobotomy McMurphy has "nothin' in the face. Just like one of those store dummies" (308). The creation of a new racial vision, purged of the crippling old associations, requires from the white American, as Kesey seems to say, the most fundamental of sacrifices.

Notes

Notes to the Introduction

1. Lawrence J. Friedman, *The White Savage: Racial Fantasies in the Postbellum South* (Englewood Cliffs, N.J.: Prentice-Hall, 1970), p. 171.

2. Thomas Dixon, Jr., *The Clansman: An Historical Romance of the Ku Klux Klan* (New York: Doubleday, Page & Co., 1905), p.312; pp. 313-14.

3. Joel Kovel, *White Racism: A Psychohistory* (New York: Random House, Pantheon Books, 1970), p.233.

4. Ibid., p. 66; p. 65.

5. James P. Comer, "White Racism: Its Root, Form, and Function," *American Journal of Psychiatry* 126 (1969): 804. Leslie A. Fiedler, in *Waiting for the End* (New York: Stein and Day, 1964), pp. 116-17, states the concept in more informal terms: "Our greatest literature has always understood what we are just beginning to come to terms with in the realm of social action: that the white Americans have, from the first, hopelessly confused the real Negroes and Indians . . . with certain projections of their own deepest minds, aspects of their own psychic life with which precisely they find it impossible to live. Here is the deepest sense in which the oppressor suffers equally with the oppressed, enslaves himself along with those who are his slaves."

6. Quoted from Charles H. Smith writing in 1893 in Claude H. Nolen, *The Negro's Image in the South: The Anatomy of White Supremacy* (Lexington: University of Kentucky Press, 1967), p. 16; Friedman, *White Savage*, p. 35.

7. Ralph Ellison, *Shadow and Act* (New York: Random House, 1964), pp. 25-26.

8. Sterling Brown, *The Image of the Negro in American Fiction* (1937;

reprint ed., Port Washington, N.Y.: Kennikat Press, 1968). They are: contented slave, wretched freeman, comic Negro, brute Negro, tragic Mulatto, local color Negro, exotic primitive.

9. Kovel, *White Racism*, p. 185.

10. C. G. Jung, "On the Psychology of the Unconscious," in *Two Essays on Analytical Psychology*, trans. R.F.C. Hull, The Collected Works of C. G. Jung, vol. 7 (1943; reprint ed., Princeton: Princeton University Press, Bollingen Series, 1972), p. 96.

11. Winthrop D. Jordan, *White Over Black: American Attitudes Toward the Negro, 1550-1812* (Chapel Hill: University of North Carolina Press, 1968), p. 24; p. 41; Harry Levin, *The Power of Blackness* (New York: Alfred A. Knopf, 1958), especially the chapter entitled "The American Nightmare."

12. Quoted in Jordan, *White Over Black*, p. 24.

13. Roy Harvey Pearce, *The Savages of America: A Study of the Indian and the Idea of Civilization* (Baltimore: Johns Hopkins University Press, 1953), p. 22; p. 15; p. 13; p. 21; p. 22.

14. J. T. Trowbridge, *Cudjo's Cave* (Boston: Lee and Shepard, 1903), p. 257; p. 258; p. 116.

15. Thomas F. Gossett, *Race: The History of an Idea in America* (Dallas: Southern Methodist University Press, 1963), p. 270.

16. Jung, "Psychology of the Unconscious," p. 68.

17. Daniel G. Hoffman, *Form and Fable in American Fiction* (New York: Oxford University Press, 1961), pp. 317-42; Kenneth S. Lynn, *Mark Twain and Southwestern Humor* (Boston: Little, Brown and Co., 1959), p.102; Leslie A. Fiedler, *Love and Death in the American Novel* (New York: Criterion Books, 1960), p. 377.

18. Maud Bodkin, *Archetypal Patterns in Poetry* (London: Oxford University Press, Humphrey Milford, 1934), p. 220; p. 229.

19. Pearce, *Savages of America*, pp. 56-57; Gossett, *Race*, p. 233.

20. Pearce, *Saveages of America*, p. 58; p.129; p. 175.

21. Friedman, *White Savage*, p. 23.

22. Charles G. Sellers, Jr., "The Travail of Slavery," in *The Southerner as*

American, ed. Charles G. Sellers, Jr. (Chapel Hill: University of North Carolina Press, 1960), p. 50.

23. Kovel, *White Racism*, pp. 91-92.

24. Catherine Juanita Starke, *Black Portraiture in American Fiction: Stock Characters, Archetypes, and Individuals* (New York: Basic Books, 1971), p. 250.

25. Stanley M. Elkins, *Slavery: A Problem in American Institutional and Intellectual Life* (Chicago: University of Chicago Press, 1959), p. 82. Studies such as Robert William Fogel and Stanley L. Engerman, *Time on the Cross: The Economics of American Negro Slavery* (Boston: Little, Brown and Co., 1974), and Eugene D. Genovese, *Roll, Jordan, Roll: The World the Slaves Made* (New York: Random House, Pantheon Books, 1974) dispute Elkins's suggestion that the Sambo stereotype had a reality stemming from antebellum plantation conditions. Genovese, for example, points out that "a Gabriel Prosser or a Nat Turner presents the opposite limiting case to the slavish personality delineated in Stanley Elkins's celebrated model," *Roll, Jordan, Roll*, p. 588. There is no doubt, however, that the image lived intensely in the white Southerner's imagination.

26. Sellers, "Travail of Slavery," p. 63; p. 52.

27. William R. Taylor, *Cavalier and Yankee: The Old South and American National Character* (New York: George Braziller, 1961, p. 151; Fogel and Engerman, *Time on the Cross*, p. 105.

28. Guy A. Cardwell, "The Plantation House: an Analogical Image," *Southern Literary Journal* 2 (1969): 14.

29. Taylor, *Cavalier and Yankee*, p. 150.

30. Hugh M. Gloster, *Negro Voices in American Fiction* (Chapel Hill: University of North Carolina Press, 1948), p. 8; p. 10.

31. Starke, *Black Portraiture*, p. 250.

32. Geroge B. Tindall, "The Central Theme Revisited," in Sellers, *Southerner as American*, p. 107; p.109.

33. C. Hugh Holman, "The Southerner as American Writer," in Sellers, *Southerner as American*, p. 181.

34. Nancy M. Tischler, *Black Masks: Negro Characters in Modern Southern Fiction* (University Park: Pennsylvania State University Press, 1969), p. 137; Thomas D. Clark, *The Emerging South* (New York: Oxford University Press,

1961), pp. 182-83; Tischler, *Black Masks*, p. 144.

35. Tischler, *Black Masks*, p. 194.

Notes to Chapter One

1. Walter Blair, *Native American Humor* (New York: American Book Co., 1937), pp. 83-84.

2. Arlin Turner, "Realism and Fantasy in Southern Humor," *Georgia Review* 12 (1958): 453.

3. Ibid.

4. Ibid., p. 454.

5. Kenneth S. Lynn, *Mark Twain and Southwestern Humor* (Boston: Little, Brown and Co., 1959), p. 52.

6. Blair, *Native American Humor*, p. 91.

7. Ibid., p. 92.

8. Lynn, *Mark Twain*, p. 64.

9. James H. Penrod, "Minority Groups in Old Southern Humor," *Southern Folklore Quarterly* 22 (1958): 123.

10. John S. Robb, *Streaks of Squatter Life* (Philadelphia: T. B. Peterson and Brothers, 1846), p. 118.

11. A. B. Longstreet, *Georgia Scenes: Characters, Incidents, &c., in the First Half Century of the Republic* (1835; reprint ed., New York: Sagamore Press, American Century Series, 1957), p. 116.

12. Joseph G. Baldwin, *The Flush Times of Alabama and Mississippi* (New York: D. Appleton and Co., 1853), p. 303.

13. Lynn, *Mark Twain*, p. 18.

14. John Q. Anderson, *Louisiana Swamp Doctor: The Life and Writings of Henry Clay Lewis* (Baton Rouge: Louisiana State University Press, 1962), p. 61. All biographical references and textual quotations are taken from this edition. As

far as is known, Lewis published twenty-five tales and five poems. All the tales and one of the poems, "The Dark Yazoo, an Indian Legend" (a romanticized Indian myth originally published January 23, 1845 in the Louisville *Journal*), are collected in Anderson's edition. Most of the tales initially appeared in William T. Porter's *Spirit of the Times*, under the signatures "Yazoo," "Tensas," or "H.C.L." Lewis collected twenty-two of the tales and published them under the pseudonym "Madison Tensas, M.D." as: *Odd Leaves from the Life of a Louisiana Swamp Doctor* (Philadelphia: A. Hart, 1850). This is the deposit volume at the Library of Congress. According to Anderson there were a number of spurious editions with inaccurate copyright dates.

The three tales published in the Anderson edition, but not in Lewis's own *Odd Leaves*, all initially appeared in the *Spirit of the Times*. They are: "Cupping on the Sternum" (1845), "Winding Up a Mississippi Bank" (1847), and "Dave Triggers' Panther" (1848). The four poems not included in Anderson's edition all appeared under the pseudonym "Ion." They are: "A Vision of Pandemonium" (a satire on the Democrats), March 29, 1844 in the Yazoo City *Whig*; "An Acrostic" (in praise of Henry Clay), August 30, 1844, in the *Whig*; "To Memory" (a serious poem), October 4, 1845 in the Louisville *Journal*; and "On the Death of D.S., who died at Matamoros—A Yazoo Volunteer," December 25, 1846 in the *Whig*.

Notes to Chapter Two

1. Charles G. Sellers, Jr., "The Travail of Slavery," in *The Southerner as American*, ed. Charles G. Sellers, Jr. (Chapel Hill: University of North Carolina Press, 1960), p. 66.

2. Guy A. Cardwell, "The Plantation House: An Analogical Image," *Southern Literary Journal* 2 (1969): 16.

3. J. V. Ridgely, *William Gilmore Simms* (New York: Twayne Publishers, 1962), p. 107.

4. Quoted in Ridgely, *William Gilmore Simms*, p. 34.

5. Ibid., p. 35; p. 36.

6. W. Gilmore Simms, *The Forayers: Or the Raid of the Dog-Days* (New York: Redfield, 1855), pp. 19-20.

7. William Gilmore Simms, *Woodcraft: Or Hawks About the Dovecote* (New York: W. J. Widdleton, 1854), p. 509, revised from *The Sword and the Distaff* (1852).

8. William Gilmore Simms, *The Yemassee: A Romance of Carolina* (New York: Harper & Brothers, 1835), 2: 225.

9. L. Moffitt Cecil, "Symbolic Pattern in *The Yemassee*," *American Literature* 35 (1964): 512.

10. William Gilmore Simms, *The Cassique of Kiawah: A Colonial Romance* (New York: Redfield, 1859), p. 18.

11. Albert Keiser, *The Indian in American Literature* (New York: Oxford University Press, 1933), p. 155.

12. William Gilmore Simms, "The Two Camps," in *The Wigwam and the Cabin* (New York: Wiley & Putnam, 1845), pp. 66-67.

13. Robert Montgomery Bird, *Nick of the Woods: Or The Jibbenainosay* (1837; reprint ed., New York: Macy-Masius, Vanguard Press, 1928), p. 219.

14. R.W.B. Lewis, *The American Adam: Innocence, Tragedy, and Tradition in the Nineteenth Century* (Chicago: University of Chicago Press, 1955), p. 109.

15. Johnson Jones Hooper, "The 'Tallapoosy Vollantares' Meet The Enemy," in *Adventures of Captain Simon Suggs* (1845; reprint ed., Chapel Hill: University of North Carolina Press, 1969), p. 105.

16. Edgar Allan Poe, *The Narrative of Arthur Gordon Pym* (1838; reprint ed., New York: Hill and Wang, 1960), p. 189.

17. Leslie A. Fiedler, *Love and Death in the American Novel* (New York: Criterion Books, 1960), p. 380.

18. Sidney Kaplan, "Introduction to *The Narrative of Arthur Gordon Pym*," in *The Narrative of Arthur Gordon Pym* (New York: Hill and Wang, 1960), p. xix; p. xxiii.

19. Joseph V. Ridgely and Iola S. Haverstick, "Chartless Voyage: The Many Narratives of *Arthur Gordon Pym*," *Texas Studies in Literature and Language* 8 (1966): 63-80.

20. Robert L. Carringer, "Circumscription of Space and the Form of Poe's *Arthur Gordon Pym*," *PMLA* 89 (1974): 506-16.

21. Ridgely and Haverstick, "Chartless Voyage," p. 80.

22. Ibid., p. 71; p. 73.

23. Joseph J. Moldenhauer, "Imagination and Perversity in *The Narrative of*

Arthur Gordon Pym," Texas Studies in Literature and Language 13 (1971): 267-68.

24. William R. Taylor, *Cavalier and Yankee: The Old South and American National Character* (New York: George Braziller, 1961), p. 191.

25. Ibid., p. 193.

26. J. V. Ridgely, *John Pendleton Kennedy* (New York: Twayne Publishers, 1966), p. 54.

27. Ibid., p. 53.

28. Jean Fagan Yellin, *The Intricate Knot: Black Figures in American Literature, 1776-1863* (New York: New York University Press, 1972), p. 53.

29. Ridgely, *John Pendleton Kennedy*, p. 58.

30. J. P. Kennedy, *Horse Shoe Robinson: A Tale of the Tory Ascendency* (Philadelphia: Carey, Lea & Blanchard, 1835), 1:66; 2:128.

31. John Pendleton Kennedy, *Swallow Barn: Or A Sojourn in the Old Dominion* (Philadelphia: Carey & Lea, 1832), 1:12.

32. Taylor, *Cavalier and Yankee*, p. 185.

33. Yellin, *Intricate Knot*, p. 58.

34. The 1832 edition of *Swallow Barn* ends with a long "Chronicle of the Life of John Smith" (II, 281-315). This romanticized account moves to restore the "beguiled" (II, 316) narrative perspective toward the South before the narrator leaves the region, for after Abe's story a long rain sets in , and there is "neither light nor shade: all the picturesque had vanished from the landscape" (II, 271).

Notes to Chapter Three

1. James H. Penrod, "The Folk Hero as Prankster in the Old Southwestern Yarns," *Kentucky Folklore Record* 2 (1956): 5.

2. Milton Rickels, *George Washington Harris* (New York: Twayne Publishers, 1965), p. 76.

3. Karl Kerényi, "The Trickster in Relation to Greek Mythology," in Paul

Radin, *The Trickster* (1956; reprint ed., New York: Greenwood Press, 1969), p. 185. The author's italics have been omitted.

4. Radin, *The Trickster*, p. ix.

5. George Washington Harris, *Sut Lovingood*, ed. Brom Weber (New York: Grove Press, 1954), p. 18. Harris's original collection of tales: George W. Harris, *Sut Lovingood. Yarns Spun by a "Nat'ral Born Durn'd Fool.["] Warped and Wove for Public Wear.* (New York: Dick & Fitzgerald, 1867), is not complete. Many of Harris's stories were published in contemporary newspapers, such as the Nashville *Union and American*. They remained scattered until recently, when a number of efforts were made to collect the yarns. The earliest is the Weber edition cited above, which includes some twenty-one tales in somewhat modernized texts. Weber mainly edits those situations where the author's phonetic humor has rendered the text confusing and difficult to follow. Wherever possible I have used this edition.

The complete stories are available in the two volumes of Harris's tales edited by M. Thomas Inge, *Sut Lovingood's Yarns* (New Haven: College and University Press, 1966) and *High Times and Hard Times* (Nashville: Vanderbilt University Press, 1967). Inge largely has retained Harris's original spelling and punctuation. Only stories from the earlier volume have been used in this chapter. They are denoted by "Inge" preceding the page number within the citation.

Many of Harris's writings were collected in the four volumes of *The Lovingood Papers* (1962-1965), edited by Ben Harris McClary. They were published by The Sut Lovingood Society, the first at Tennessee Wesleyan College, Athens, and the following three by the University of Tennessee Press, Knoxville.

6. Lewis Leary, *Southern Excursions: Essays on Mark Twain and Others* (Baton Rouge: Louisiana State University Press, 1971), p. 112.

7. Radin, *Trickster*, p.185.

8. When asked to name his favorite fictional characters, William Faulkner replied: "And then I like Sut Lovingood, from a book written by George Harris about 1840 or '50 in the Tennessee mountains. He had no illusions about himself, did the best he could; at certain times he was a coward and knew it and wasn't ashamed; he never blamed his misfortunes on anyone and never cursed God for them." The quote appears in Malcolm Cowley, ed. *Writers at Work* (1959; reprint ed., New York: Viking Press, 1965), p. 137. M. Thomas Inge discusses evidence of Faulkner's awareness of Harris's work in *As I Lay Dying* in his "William Faulkner and George Washington Harris," *Tennessee Studies in Literature* 6 (1962): 47-59. William Van O'Conner discusses similar evidence in "Spotted Horses" in his *The Tangled Fire of William Faulkner* (Minneapolis: University of Minnesota Press, 1954), p. 123. Mark Twain too knew of Harris's *Yarns*, having reviewed them for the San Francisco *Alta California* (July 14, 1867). Walter Blair, *Mark Twain and Huck Finn* (Berkeley and Los Angeles: University of California Press, 1960), pp. 242-43, suggests Twain had Harris on

his mind during some of the writing of *Huckleberry Finn*. E. Hudson Long, "Sut Lovingood and Mark Twain's *Joan of Arc,*" *Modern Language Notes* 64 (1949): 37-39, and D. M. McKeithan, "Mark Twain's Story of the Bull and the Bees," *Tennessee Historical Quarterly* 11 (1952): 246-53, also discuss Harris's influence on Twain's fiction.

9. F. O. Matthiessen, *American Renaissance: Art and Expression in the Age of Emerson and Whitman* (New York: Oxford University Press, 1941), p. 644.

10. Kenneth S. Lynn, *Mark Twain and Southwestern Humor* (Boston: Little, Brown and Co., 1959), p. 131.

11. Eugene Current-Garcia, "Sut Lovingood's Rare Ripe Southern Garden," *Studies in Short Fiction* 9 (1972): 117.

12. Rickels, *George Washington Harris*, p. 27.

13. Ibid., p. 70.

14. Ibid., p. 117.

15. Harris emphatically shared the South's hostile attitudes toward the Negro and Indian. As Rickels points out, he was an avid supporter of slavery, opposing the more moderate views of his East Tennessee home. When he could afford it, Harris kept black slaves, adhering even to the custom of buying a Negro infant to grow up with his first born son as servant. Furthermore, one of Harris's many jobs brought about direct involvement with the cruelest phase of Indian Removal. As a steamboat captain on the Tennessee River in 1838, Harris "took part in the genocidal forced removal of the Cherokees, when they were driven from their ancestral lands and transported, some by river boat, to regions west of the Mississippi." According to Rickels, one of the local legends surviving about him depicts Harris denying the Indians the comfort of whiskey on their tragic journey, p. 21.

16. Walter Blair, *Native American Humor* (New York: American Book Company, 1937), p. 99.

17. Lynn, *Mark Twain*, p. 133.

Notes to Chapter Four

1. Kenneth S. Lynn, *Mark Twain and Southwestern Humor* (Boston: Little, Brown and Co., 1959), p. 143.

2. Dixon Wecter, *Sam Clemens of Hannibal* (Boston: Houghton Mifflin Co., 1952), p. 45.

3. Arthur G. Pettit, *Mark Twain and the South* (Lexington: University Press of Kentucky, 1974), p. 9.

4. Justin Kaplan, *Mr. Clemens and Mark Twain* (New York: Simon and Schuster, 1966), p. 256.

5. Ibid., pp. 255-56.

6. Pettit, *Mark Twain and the South*, p. 5. As Pettit puts it elsewhere, "Quite clearly, outside pressures forced Clemens, occasionally against his will, to conform to certain environmental conditions, "Mark Twain and the Negro, 1867-1869," *Journal of Negro History* 56 (1971): 95.

7. Helen L. Harris, "Mark Twain's Response to the Native American," *American Literature* 46 (1975): 495.

8. Mark Twain, *Roughing It, The Writings of Mark Twain* (New York: Harper & Brothers, 1907-1918), 7:157. Following the precedent set by James M. Cox in *Mark Twain: The Fate of Humor* (Princeton: Princeton University Press, 1966), unless otherwise noted, all references to Mark Twain's works will be to this easily available Author's National Edition. Franklin R. Rogers, ed., *The Pattern for Mark Twain's Roughing It: Letters from Nevada by Samuel and Orion Clemens, 1861-1862* (Berkeley and Los Angeles: University of California Press, 1961), p. 38; *Mark Twain Papers*, DeVoto, 326, quoted in Wecter, *Sam Clemens*, p. 151.

9. Mark Twain, *The Adventures of Tom Sawyer, The Writings of Mark Twain* (New York: Harper & Brothers, 1907-1918), 12: 259.

10. Lynn, *Mark Twain*, p. 195; Robert Tracy, "Myth and Reality in *The Adventures of Tom Sawyer,*" *Southern Review*, n.s. 4 (1968): 537; Lewis Leary, *Southern Excursions: Essays on Mark Twain and Others* (Baton Rouge:Louisiana State University Press, 1971), p. 102; Leslie A. Fiedler, *Love and Death in the American Novel* (New York: Criterion Books, 1960), p. 570; Bernard DeVoto, Introduction to *The Portable Mark Twain* (New York: Viking Press, 1946), p. 33.

11. James M. Cox, *Mark Twain: The Fate of Humor* (Princeton: Princeton University Press, 1966), p. 131; p. 147.

12. Ibid., p. 148.

13. Daniel G. Hoffman, *Form and Fable in American Fiction* (New York: Oxford University Press, 1961), p. 325.

14. Leary, *Southern Excursions*, p. 101; Walter Blair, "On the Structure of *Tom Sawyer*," *Modern Philology* 37 (1939): 84.

15. Walter Blair, *Mark Twain and Huck Finn* (Berkeley and Los Angeles: University of California Press, 1960), p. 58.

16. Mark Twain, *The Autobiography of Mark Twain*, ed. Charles Neider (New York: Harper and Row, 1959), p. 68.

17. Wecter, *Sam Clemens*, pp. 160-61.

18. Tracy, "Myth and Reality," p. 536

19. Henry Nash Smith, *Mark Twain: The Development of a Writer* (Cambridge: Harvard University Press, Belknap Press, 1962), p. 84.

20. Tracy, "Myth and Reality," p. 539.

21. Twain, *Autobiography*, p. 43.

22. Walt Whitman, *Leaves of Grass: Comprehensive Reader's Edition*, eds., Harold W. Blodgett and Sculley Bradley (New York: New York University Press, 1965), p. 251, 1. 136.

23. Twain, *Autobiography*, p. 9.

Notes to Chapter Five

1. Henry Nash Smith, *Mark Twain: The Development of a Writer* (Cambridge: Harvard University Press, Belknap Press, 1962), p. 137.

2. Chadwick Hansen, "The Character of Jim and the Ending of *Huckleberry Finn*," *Massachusetts Review* 5 (1963): 59-60.

3. James M. Cox, *Mark Twain: The Fate of Humor* (Princeton: Princeton University Press, 1966), p. 180.

4. Smith, *Development of a Writer*, p. 132.

5. Leo Marx, "Mr. Eliot, Mr. Trilling, and *Huckleberry Finn*," *American Scholar* 22 (1953): 432.

6. Hansen, "Character of Jim," p. 60.

7. Ibid., p. 55.

8. Smith, *Development of a Writer*, p. 114.

9. Neil Schmitz, "Twain, *Huckleberry Finn*, and the Reconstruction," *American Studies* 12 (1971): 61.

10. Mark Twain, *The Adventures of Huckleberry Finn, The Writings of Mark Twain* (New York: Harper & Brothers, 1907-1918), 13: 18.

11. Daniel G. Hoffman, *Form and Fable in American Fiction* (New York: Oxford University Press, 1961), p. 331.

12. Ibid., p. 335.

13. *Adventures of Huckleberry Finn*, ed. Leo Marx (Indianapolis: Bobbs-Merrill Co., 1967), p. 56n.

14. Neil Schmitz, "The Paradox of Liberation in *Huckleberry Finn*," *Texas Studies in Literature and Language* 13 (1971): 131.

15. Alan Trachtenberg, "The Form of Freedom in *Adventures of Huckleberry Finn*," *Southern Review*, n.s. 6 (1970): 968.

16. Smith, *Development of a Writer*, p. 123.

17. Hansen, "Character of Jim," p. 56.

18. *Huckleberry Finn*, ed. Leo Marx, p. 142n.

19. Hoffman, *Form and Fable*, p. 321.

20. Kenneth S. Lynn, *Mark Twain and Southwestern Humor* (Boston: Little, Brown and Co., 1959), p. 220.

21. Smith, *Development of a Writer*, p. 118.

22. Victor A. Doyno, "Over Twain's Shoulder: The Composition and Structure of *Huckleberry Finn*," *Modern Fiction Studies* 14 (1968): 8.

23. Hansen, "Character of Jim," pp. 59-60.

24. Lynn, *Mark Twain*, p. 238.

25. Smith, *Development of a Writer*, p. 184.

26. Stanley Brodwin, "Blackness and the Adamic Myth in Mark Twain's *Pudd'nhead Wilson*," *Texas Studies in Literature and Language* 15 (1973): 175.

27. Mark Twain, *Pudd'nhead Wilson, The Writings of Mark Twain* (New York: Harper & Brothers, 1907-1918), 14: 224.

28. James M. Cox, "*Pudd'nhead Wilson:* The End of Mark Twain's American Dream," *South Atlantic Quarterly* 58 (1959): 355.

29. Ibid.

30. Ibid., p. 357.

31. Smith, *Development of a Writer*, p. 181.

32. Leslie A. Fiedler, " 'As Free as Any Cretur . . .' II," *New Republic*, August 22, 1955, p. 17.

33. From a letter of July 30, 1893 to Fred J. Hall, *Mark Twain's Letters*, ed. Albert Bigelow Paine (New York: Harper & Brothers, 1917), 2: 591; quoted also in Brodwin, "Blackness and the Adamic Myth," p. 168.

Notes to Chapter Six

1. Arthur F. Kinney, "Faulkner and the Possibilities for Heroism," in *Bear, Man, and God, Eight Approaches to William Faulkner's "The Bear,"* eds., Francis Lee Utley, Lynn Z. Bloom, and Arthur F. Kinney (New York: Random House, 1971), p. 247.

2. Lewis M. Dabney, *The Indians of Yoknapatawpha: A Study in Literature and History* (Baton Rouge: Louisiana State University Press, 1974), p. 10.

3. William Faulkner, "Red Leaves," in *Selected Short Stories of William Faulkner* (New York: Random House, Modern Library, 1961), pp. 101-2; p. 116.

4. William Faulkner, "The Old People," in *Go Down, Moses* (New York: Random House, 1942), p. 173.

5. Ibid., p. 167.

6. Faulkner, "The Bear," in *Go Down, Moses*, p. 215.

7. Faulkner, "The Old People," p. 165.

8. Ibid.

9. Faulkner, "The Bear," p. 246.

10. Ibid., p. 300.

11. Francis Lee Utley, "Pride and Humility: The Cultural Roots of Ike McCaslin," in *Bear, Man, and God*, p. 187.

12. Kinney, "Faulkner and Heroism," p. 247.

13. T. H. Adamowski, "Isaac McCaslin and the Wilderness of the Imagination," *Centennial Review* 17 (1973): 98.

14. Utley, "Pride and Humility," p. 185.

15. Robert Penn Warren, "Faulkner: The South and the Negro," *Southern Review*, n.s. 1 (1965): 520.

16. Irene C. Edmonds, "Faulkner and the Black Shadow," in *Southern Renascence: The Literature of the Modern South*, eds., Louis D. Rubin, Jr. and Robert D. Jacobs (Baltimore: The Johns Hopkins University Press, 1953), p. 202.

17. Walter Taylor, "Faulkner's Pantaloon: The Negro Anomaly at the Heart of *Go Down, Moses*," *American Literature* 44 (1972): 432-33.

18. Ibid., p. 432.

19. Ralph Ellison, *Shadow and Act* (New York: Random House, 1964), p. 42.

20. Charles H. Nilon, *Faulkner and the Negro* (New York: Citadel Press, 1965), p. 33.

21. Taylor, "Faulkner's Pantaloon," p. 437.

22. Irving Howe, *William Faulkner: A Critical Study* (New York: Vintage Books, 1952), p. 128.

23. Alfred Kazin, "The Stillness of *Light in August*," in *Twelve Original Essays on Great American Novels*, ed. Charles Shapiro (Detroit: Wayne State University Press, 1958), p. 260.

24. Faulkner, "Red Leaves," p. 104.

25. Faulkner, "Pantaloon in Black," in *Go Down, Moses*, p. 159.

26. Nilon, *Faulkner and the Negro*, p. 37.

27. Olga W. Vickery, *The Novels of William Faulkner: A Critical Interpretation* (Baton Rouge: Louisiana State University Press, 1964), p. 68.

28. Richard Chase, *The American Novel and Its Tradition* (Garden City, New York: Doubleday and Co., Anchor Books, 1957), pp. 213-14.

29. Kazin, "Stillness of *Light in August*," p. 263.

30. William Faulkner, *Light in August* (New York: Random House, 1932), p. 356.

31. Vickery, *Novels of William Faulkner*, pp. 73-74.

32. Kazin, "Stillness of *Light in August*," p. 271.

Notes to the Conclusion

1. Louise Y. Gossett, *Violence in Recent Southern Fiction* (Durham, N.C.: Duke University Press, 1965), p. 20; p. 193.

2. Elizabeth Spencer, *The Voice at the Back Door* (New York: McGraw-Hill Book Co., 1956), p. 25.

3. Eunice Glenn, "Fantasy in the Fiction of Eudora Welty," in *Critiques and Essays on Modern Fiction: 1920-1951*, ed. John W. Aldridge (New York: Ronald Press Co., 1952), p. 512; John Hawkes, "Flannery O'Connor's Devil," *Sewannee Review* 70 (1962): 395.

4. Frederick J. Hoffman, *The Art of Southern Fiction: A Study of Some Modern Novelists* (Carbondale: Southern Illinois University Press, 1967), p. 10.

5. Paschal Reeves, *Thomas Wolfe's Albatross: Race and Nationality in America* (Athens: University of Georgia Press, 1968), p. 34.

6. Thomas Wolfe, *The Web and the Rock* (New York: Harper & Row, 1937), p. 143.

7. Gossett, *Recent Southern Fiction*, p. 12.

8. Ihab Hassan, *Radical Innocence: Studies in The Contemporary American Novel* (Princeton: Princeton University Press, 1961), p. 212.

9. Carson McCullers, *The Heart is a Lonely Hunter* (Boston: Houghton Mifflin Co., Riverside Press, 1940), p. 63.

10. Martha Stephens, *The Question of Flannery O'Connor* (Baton Rouge: Louisiana State University Press, 1973), p. 68; Preston M. Browning, Jr., *Flannery O'Connor* (Carbondale: Southern Illinois University Press, 1974), p. 29.

11. Stephens, *Question of Flannery O'Connor*, p. 66.

12. Besides the implication in Stephens's discussion, Browning suggests that "using material from short stories written earlier, she apparently encountered a good deal of difficulty plotting a strategy for the final version," *Flannery O'Connor–*, p. 25.

13. Kathleen Feeley, *Flannery O'Connor: Voice of the Peacock* (New Brunswick, N. J.: Rutgers University Press, 1972), p. 66.

14. Hawkes, "Flannery O'Connor's Devil," p. 401.

15. Flannery O'Connor, *Wise Blood* (New York: Farrar, Straus and Giroux, 1949), p. 197.

16. Flannery O'Connor, "The Artificial Nigger," in *A Good Man is Hard to Find* (New York: Harcourt, Brace & World, 1953), pp. 108-9.

17. Gilbert Muller, "The City of Woe: Flannery O'Connor's Dantean Vision," *Georgia Review* 23 (1969): 212.

18. Ibid., p. 210.

19. Browning, *Flannery O'Connor*, p. 67.

20. Muller, "City of Woe," p. 212.

21. Herman Melville, *Moby-Dick*, eds., Harrison Hayford and Hershel Parker (New York: W. W. Norton & Co., 1967), p. 53; p. 399.

22. Quoted in Hawkes, "Flannery O'Connor's Devil," p. 395.

23. Nathaniel Hawthorne, "My Kinsman, Major Molineux," in *The Complete Novels and Selected Tales of Nathaniel Hawthorne*, ed. Norman Holmes Pearson (New York: Random House, Modern Library, 1937), p. 1216; p. 1221.

24. Nathaniel Hawthorne, *The Blithedale Romance, The Centenary Edition of the Works of Nathaniel Hawthorne*, (Columbus: Ohio State University Press, 1964), 3: 91; p. 92.

25. Gossett, *Recent Southern Fiction*, p. 184.

26. Shirley Ann Grau, *The Black Prince and Other Stories* (New York: Alfred A. Knopf, 1955), p. 48.

27. Gossett, *Recent Southern Fiction*, p. 188.

28. William Styron, *Lie Down in Darkness* (Indianapolis: Bobbs-Merrill Co., 1951), p. 393.

29. Gossett, *Recent Southern Fiction*, p. 127.

30. Eudora Welty, "A Worn Path," along with "Powerhouse" and "Keela, the Outcast Indian Maiden," in *A Curtain of Green And Other Stories* (New York: Harcourt, Brace & World, 1936), p. 276.

31. Ruth M. Vande Kieft, *Eudora Welty* (New York: Twayne Publishers, 1962), p. 83.

32. Glenn, "Fiction of Eudora Welty," p. 512.

33. Gossett, *Recent Southern Fiction*, p. 109.

34. Joyce B. Markle, *Fighters and Lovers: Theme in the Novels of John Updike* (New York: New York University Press, 1973), p. 160; p. 159.

35. John Updike, *Rabbit Redux* (New York: Alfred A. Knopf, 1971), p. 125.

36. Norman Mailer, *An American Dream* (New York: Dial Press, 1965), p. 182.

37. Barry H. Leeds, *The Structured Vision of Norman Mailer* (New York: New York University Press, 1969), p. 144; p. 148.

38. Ibid., p. 168.

39. Thomas Pynchon, *Gravity's Rainbow* (New York: Viking Press, 1973), p. 316.

40. Ken Kesey, *One Flew Over the Cuckoo's Nest* (New York: Viking Press, 1962), p. 28.

41. Terence Martin, ''*One Flew Over the Cuckoo's Nest* and the High Cost of Living,'' *Modern Fiction Studies* 19 (1973): 45.

42. Ibid., p. 43.

43. Ibid., p. 48.

Bibliography

Adamowski, T. H. "Isaac McCaslin and the Wilderness of the Imagination." *Centennial Review* 17 (1973): 92-112.

Anderson, John Q. *Louisiana Swamp Doctor: The Life and Writings of Henry Clay Lewis*. Baton Rouge: Louisiana State University Press, 1962.

Baldwin, Joseph G. *The Flush Times of Alabama and Mississippi*. New York: D. Appleton and Co., 1853.

Bird, Robert Montgomery. *Nick of the Woods: Or The Jibbenainosay*. 1837. Reprint. New York: Macy-Masius, Vanguard Press, 1928.

Blair, Walter. *Mark Twain and Huck Finn*. Berkeley and Los Angeles: University of California Press, 1960.

——. *Native American Humor*. New York: American Book Co., 1937.

——. "On the Structure of *Tom Sawyer*." *Modern Philology* 37 (1939): 75-88.

Bodkin, Maud. *Archetypal Patterns in Poetry*. London: Oxford University Press, Humphrey Milford, 1934.

Brodwin, Stanley. "Blackness and the Adamic Myth in Mark Twain's *Pudd'nhead Wilson*." *Texas Studies in Literature and Language* 15 (1973): 167-76.

Brown, Sterling. *The Image of the Negro in American Fiction*. 1937. Reprint. Port Washington, N.Y.: Kennikat Press, 1968.

Browning, Preston M., Jr. *Flannery O'Connor*. Carbondale: Southern Illinois University Press, 1974.

Cardwell, Guy A. "The Plantation House: An Analogical Image." *Southern Literary Journal* 2 (1969): 3-21.

Carringer, Robert L. "Circumscription of Space and the Form of Poe's *Arthur Gordon Pym.*" *PMLA* 89 (1974): 506-16.

Cecil, L. Moffitt. "Symbolic Pattern in *The Yemassee.*" *American Literature* 35 (1964): 510-14.

Chase, Richard. *The American Novel and Its Tradition.* Garden City, N.Y.: Doubleday and Co., Anchor Books, 1957.

Clark, Thomas D. *The Emerging South.* New York: Oxford University Press, 1961.

Clemens, Samuel L. *The Adventures of Huckleberry Finn.* The Writings of Mark Twain. Author's National Edition, vol. 13. New York: Harper & Brothers, 1907-1918.

———. *The Adventures of Tom Sawyer.* The Writings of Mark Twain. Author's National Edition, vol. 12. New York: Harper & Brothers, 1907-1918.

———. *The Autobiography of Mark Twain.* Edited by Charles Neider. New York: Harper and Row, 1959.

———. *Mark Twain's Letters.* Edited by Albert Bigelow Paine. 2 vols. New York: Harper & Brothers, 1917.

———. *Pudd'nhead Wilson.* The Writings of Mark Twain. Author's National Edition, vol. 14. New York: Harper & Brothers, 1907-1918.

———. *Roughing It.* The Writings of Mark Twain. Author's National Edition, vol 7. New York: Harper & Brothers, 1907-1918.

Clemens, Samuel L. and Clemens, Orion. *The Pattern for Mark Twain's Roughing It: Letters from Nevada by Samuel and Orion Clemens, 1861-1862.* Edited by Franklin R. Rogers. Berkeley and Los Angeles: University of California Press, 1961.

Comer, James P. "White Racism: Its Root, Form, and Function." *American Journal of Psychiatry* 126 (1969): 802-06.

Cowley, Malcom, ed. *Writers at Work.* 1959. Reprint. New York: Viking Press, 1965.

Cox, James M. *Mark Twain: The Fate of Humor.* Princeton: Princeton University Press, 1966.

———. "*Pudd'nhead Wilson*: The End of Mark Twain's American Dream." *South Atlantic Quarterly* 58 (1959): 351-63.

Current-Garcia, Eugene. "Sut Lovingood's Rare Ripe Southern Garden." *Studies in Short Fiction* 9 (1972): 117-29.

Dabney, Lewis M. *The Indians of Yoknapatawpha: A Study in Literature and History.* Baton Rouge: Louisiana State University Press, 1974.

DeVoto, Bernard. Introduction to *The Portable Mark Twain*. New York: Viking Press, 1946.

Dixon, Thomas, Jr. *The Clansman: An Historical Romance of the Ku Klux Klan*. New York: Doubleday, Page & Co., 1905.

Doyno, Victor A. "Over Twain's Shoulder: The Composition and Structure of *Huckleberry Finn*." *Modern Fiction Studies* 14 (1968): 3-9.

Edmonds, Irene C. "Faulkner and the Black Shadow." In *Southern Renascence: The Literature of the Modern South*, edited by Louis D. Rubin, Jr. and Robert D. Jacobs. Baltimore: Johns Hopkins University Press, 1953.

Elkins, Stanley M. *Slavery: A Problem in American Institutional and Intellectual Life*. Chicago: University of Chicago Press, 1959.

Ellison, Ralph. *Shadow and Act*. New York: Random House, 1964.

Faulkner, William. "The Bear." In *Go Down, Moses*. 1942. New York: Random House, Modern Library, 1955.

———. *Light in August*. 1932. New York: Random House, Modern Library, 1959.

———. "The Old People." In *Go Down, Moses*. 1942. New York: Random House, Modern Library, 1955.

———. "Pantaloon in Black." In *Go Down, Moses*. 1942. New York: Random House, Modern Library, 1955.

———. "Red Leaves." In *Selected Short Stories of William Faulkner*. New York: Random House, Modern Library, 1961.

Feeley, Kathleen. *Flannery O'Connor: The Voice of the Peacock*. New Brunswick, N.J.: Rutgers University Press, 1972.

Fiedler, Leslie A. " 'As Free as Any Cretur . . .' II." *New Republic*, 22 August 1955, p. 17.

———. *Love and Death in the American Novel*. New York: Criterion Books, 1960.

———. *Waiting for the End*. New York: Stein and Day, 1964.

Fogel, Robert William and Engerman, Stanley L. *Time on the Cross: The Economics of American Negro Slavery*. Boston: Little, Brown and Co., 1974.

Friedman, Lawrence J. *The White Savage: Racial Fantasies in the Postbellum South*. Englewood Cliffs, N.J.: Prentice-Hall, 1970.

Genovese, Eugene D. *Roll, Jordan, Roll: The World the Slaves Made*. New York: Random House, Pantheon Books, 1974.

Glenn, Eunice. "Fantasy in the Fiction of Eudora Welty," In *Critiques and Essays on Modern Fiction: 1920-1951*, edited by John W. Aldridge. New York: Ronald Press Co., 1952.

Gloster, Hugh M. *Negro Voices in American Fiction.* Chapel Hill: University of North Carolina Press, 1948.

Gossett, Louise Y. *Violence in Recent Southern Fiction.* Durham, N.C.: Duke University Press, 1965.

Gossett, Thomas F. *Race: The History of an Idea in America.* Dallas: Southern Methodist University Press, 1963.

Grau, Shirley Ann. *The Black Prince and Other Stories.* 1955. New York: Alfred A. Knopf, 1968.

Hansen, Chadwick. "The Character of Jim and the Ending of *Huckleberry Finn.*" *Massachusetts Review* 5 (1963): 45-66.

Harris, George Washington. *High Times and Hard Times.* Edited by M. Thomas Inge. Nashville: Vanderbilt University Press 1967.

———. *Sut Lovingood.* Edited by Brom Weber. New York: Grove Press, 1954.

———. *Sut Lovingood. Yarns Spun by a "Nat'ral Born Durn'd Fool.["] Warped and Wove for Public Wear.* New York: Dick & Fitzgerald, 1867.

———. *Sut Lovingood's Yarns.* Edited by M. Thomas Inge. New Haven: College and University Press, 1966.

Harris, Helen L. "Mark Twain's Response to the Native American." *American Literature* 46 (1975): 495-505.

Hassan, Ihab. *Radical Innocence: Studies in The Contemporary American Novel.* Princeton: Princeton University Press, 1961.

Hawkes, John. "Flannery O'Connor's Devil." *Sewannee Review* 70 (1962): 395-407.

Hawthorne, Nathaniel. *The Blithedale Romance.* The Centenary Edition of the Works of Nathaniel Hawthorne, vol. 3. Columbus: Ohio State University Press, 1964.

———. "My Kinsman, Major Molineux." In *The Complete Novels and Selected Tales of Nathaniel Hawthorne.* Edited by Norman Holmes Pearson. New York: Random House, Modern Library, 1937.

Hoffman, Daniel G. *Form and Fable in American Fiction.* New York: Oxford University Press, 1961.

Hoffman, Frederick J. *The Art of Southern Fiction: A Study of Some Modern Novelists.* Carbondale: Southern Illinois University Press, 1967.

Holman, C. Hugh. "The Southerner as American Writer." In *The Southerner as American,* edited by Charles G. Sellers, Jr. Chapel Hill: University of North Carolina Press, 1960.

Hooper, Johnson Jones. "The 'Tallapoosy Vollantares' Meet The Enemy." In *Adventures of Captain Simon Suggs*. 1845. Reprint. Chapel Hill: University of North Carolina Press, 1969.

Howe, Irving. *William Faulkner: A Critical Study*. New York: Vintage Books, 1952.

Inge, M. Thomas. "William Faulkner and George Washington Harris." *Tennessee Studies in Literature* 6 (1962): 47-59.

Jordan, Winthrop D. *White Over Black: American Attitudes Toward the Negro, 1550-1812*. Chapel Hill: University of North Carolina Press, 1968.

Jung, C. G. "On the Psychology of the Unconscious." In *Two Essays on Analytical Psychology*. Translated by R.F.C. Hull. The Collected Works of C. G. Jung, vol. 7. 1943. Reprint. Princeton: Princeton University Press, Bollingen Series, 1972.

Kaplan, Justin. *Mr. Clemens and Mark Twain*. New York: Simon and Schuster, 1966.

Kazin, Alfred. "The Stillness of *Light in August*." In *Twelve Original Essays on Great American Novels*, edited by Charles Shapiro. Detroit: Wayne State University Press, 1958.

Keiser, Albert. *The Indian in American Literature*. New York: Oxford University Press, 1933.

Kennedy, J. P. *Horse Shoe Robinson: A Tale of the Tory Ascendency*. 2 vols. Philadelphia: Carey, Lea & Blanchard, 1835.

Kennedy, John Pendleton. *Rob of the Bowl: A Legend of St. Inigoe's*. 2 vols. Philadelphia: Lea & Blanchard, 1838.

———. *Swallow Barn: Or A Sojourn in the Old Dominion*. 2 vols. Philadelphia: Carey & Lea, 1832.

Kesey, Ken. *One Flew Over the Cuckoo's Nest*. New York: Viking Press, 1962.

Vande Kieft, Ruth M. *Eudora Welty*. New York: Twayne Publishers, 1962.

Kinney, Arthur F. "Faulkner and the Possibilities for Heroism." In *Bear, Man, and God: Eight Approaches to William Faulkner's "The Bear,"* edited by Francis Lee Utley, Lynn Z. Bloom, and Arthur F. Kinney. New York: Random House, 1971.

Kovel, Joel. *White Racism: A Psychohistory*. New York: Random House, Pantheon Books, 1970.

Leary, Lewis. *Southern Excursions: Essays on Mark Twain and Others*. Baton Rouge: Louisiana State University Press, 1971.

Leeds, Barry H. *The Structured Vision of Norman Mailer*. New York: New York University Press, 1969.

Levin, Harry. *The Power of Blackness*. New York: Alfred A. Knopf, 1958.

Lewis, R.W.B. *The American Adam: Innocence Tragedy and Tradition in the Nineteenth Century*. Chicago: University of Chicago Press, 1955.

Long, E. Hudson. "Sut Lovingood and Mark Twain's *Joan of Arc.*" *Modern Language Notes* 64 (1949): 37-39.

Longstreet, A. B. *Georgia Scenes: Characters, Incidents, &c., in the First Half Century of the Republic*. 1835. Reprint. New York: Sagamore Press, American Century Series, 1957.

Lynn, Kenneth S. *Mark Twain and Southwestern Humor*. Boston: Little, Brown and Co., 1959.

Mailer, Norman. *An American Dream*. New York: Dial Press, 1965.

Markle, Joyce B. *Fighters and Lovers: Theme in the Novels of John Updike*. New York: New York University Press, 1973.

Martin, Terence. "*One Flew Over the Cuckoo's Nest* and the High Cost of Living." *Modern Fiction Studies* 19 (1973): 43-55.

Marx, Leo, ed. *Adventures of Huckleberry Finn*. Indianapolis: Bobbs-Merrill Co., 1967.

————. "Mr. Eliot, Mr. Trilling, and *Huckleberry Finn.*" *American Scholar* 22 (1953): 423-40.

Matthiessen, F. O. *American Renaissance: Art and Expression in the Age of Emerson and Whitman*. New York: Oxford University Press, 1941.

McCullers, Carson. *The Heart is a Lonely Hunter*. Boston: Houghton Mifflin Co., Riverside Press, 1940.

Melville, Herman. *Moby-Dick*. Edited by Harrison Hayford and Hershel Parker. New York: W. W. Norton & Co., 1967.

McKeithan, D. M. "Mark Twain's Story of the Bull and the Bees." *Tennessee Historical Quarterly* 11 (1952): 246-53.

Moldenhauer, Joseph J. "Imagination and Perversity in *The Narrative of Arthur Gordon Pym.*" *Texas Studies in Literature and Language* 13 (1971): 267-80.

Muller, Gilbert. "The City of Woe: Flannery O'Connor's Dantean Vision." *Georgia Review* 23 (1969): 206-13.

Nilon, Charles H. *Faulkner and the Negro*. New York: Citadel Press, 1965.

Nolen, Claude H. *The Negro's Image in the South: The Anatomy of White Supremacy*. Lexington: University of Kentucky Press, 1967.

O'Conner, William Van. *The Tangled Fire of William Faulkner*. Minneapolis: University of Minnesota Press, 1954.

O'Connor, Flannery. "The Artificial Nigger." In *A Good Man is Hard to Find*. New York: Harcourt, Brace & World, 1953.

———. *Wise Blood*. New York: Farrar, Straus and Giroux, 1949.

Pearce, Roy Harvey. *The Savages of America: A Study of the Indian and the Idea of Civilization*. Baltimore: Johns Hopkins University Press, 1953.

Penrod, James H. "The Folk Hero as Prankster in the Old Southwestern Yarns." *Kentucky Folklore Record* 2 (1956): 5-12.

———. "Minority Groups in Old Southern Humor." *Southern Folklore Quarterly* 22 (1958): 121-28.

Pettit, Arthur G. "Mark Twain and the Negro, 1867-1869." *Journal of Negro History* 56 (1971): 88-96.

———. *Mark Twain and the South*. Lexington, Ky.: University Press of Kentucky, 1974.

Poe, Edgar Allan. *The Narrative of Arthur Gordon Pym*. Edited by Sidney Kaplan. New York: Hill and Wang, 1960.

Pynchon, Thomas. *Gravity's Rainbow*. New York: Viking Press, 1973.

Radin, Paul. *The Trickster*. 1956. Reprint. New York: Greenwood Press, 1969.

Reeves, Paschal. *Thomas Wolfe's Albatross: Race and Nationality in America*. Athens: University of Georgia Press, 1968.

Rickels, Milton. *George Washington Harris*. New York: Twayne Publishers, 1965.

Ridgely, J. V. *John Pendleton Kennedy*. New York: Twayne Publishers, 1966.

———. *William Gilmore Simms*. New York: Twayne Publishers, 1962.

Ridgely, Joseph V. and Haverstick, Iola S. "Chartless Voyage: The Many Narratives of *Arthur Gordon Pym*." *Texas Studies in Literature and Language* 8 (1966): 63-80.

Robb, John S. *Streaks of Squatter Life*. Philadelphia: T. B. Peterson and Brothers, 1846.

Schmitz, Neil. "The Paradox of Liberation in *Huckleberry Finn*." *Texas Studies in Literature and Language* 13 (1971): 125-36.

———. "Twain, *Huckleberry Finn*, and the Reconstruction." *American Studies* 12 (1971): 59-67.

Sellers, Charles G., Jr. "The Travail of Slavery." In *The Southerner as American*, edited by Charles G. Sellers, Jr. Chapel Hill: University of North Carolina Press, 1960.

Simms, William Gilmore. *The Cassique of Kiawah: A Colonial Romance*. New York: Redfield, 1859.

Simms, W. Gilmore. *The Forayers: Or the Raid of the Dog-Days*. New York: Redfield, 1855.

Simms, William Gilmore. "The Two Camps." In *The Wigwam and the Cabin*. New York: Wiley & Putnam, 1845.

———. *Woodcraft: Or Hawks About the Dovecote*. New York: W. J. Widdleton, 1854.

———. *The Yemassee: A Romance of Carolina*. 2 vols. New York: Harper & Brothers, 1835.

Smith, Henry Nash. *Mark Twain: The Development of a Writer*. Cambridge: Harvard University Press, Belknap Press, 1962.

Spencer, Elizabeth. *The Voice at the Back Door*. New York: McGraw-Hill Book Co., 1956.

Starke, Catherine Juanita. *Black Portraiture in American Fiction: Stock Characters, Archetypes, and Individuals*. New York: Basic Books, 1971.

Stephens, Martha. *The Question of Flannery O'Connor*. Baton Rouge: Louisiana State University Press, 1973.

Styron, William. *Lie Down in Darkness*. Indianapolis: Bobbs-Merrill Co., 1951.

Taylor, Walter. "Faulkner's Pantaloon: The Negro Anomaly at the Heart of *Go Down, Moses*." *American Literature* 44 (1972): 430-44.

Taylor, William R. *Cavalier and Yankee: The Old South and American National Character*. New York: George Braziller, 1961.

Tindall, George B. "The Central Theme Revisited." In *The Southerner as American*, edited by Charles G. Sellers, Jr. Chapel Hill: University of North Carolina Press, 1960.

Tischler, Nancy M. *Black Masks: Negro Characters in Modern Southern Fiction*. University Park: Pennsylvania State University Press, 1969.

Trachtenberg, Alan. "The Form of Freedom in *Adventures of Huckleberry Finn*." *Southern Review*, n.s. 6 (1970): 954-71.

Tracy, Robert. "Myth and Reality in *The Adventures of Tom Sawyer*." *Southern Review*, n.s. 4 (1968): 530-41.

Trowbridge, J. T. *Cudjo's Cave*. 1863. Boston: Lee and Shepard, 1903.

Turner, Arlin. "Realism and Fantasy in Southern Humor." *Georgia Review* 12 (1958): 451-57.

Updike, John. *Rabbit Redux*. New York: Alfred A. Knopf, 1971.

Utley, Francis Lee. "Pride and Humility: The Cultural Roots of Ike McCaslin." In *Bear, Man, and God: Eight Approaches to William Faulkner's "The Bear,"* edited by Francis Lee Utley, Lynn Z. Bloom, and Arthur F. Kinney. New York: Random House, 1971.

Vickery, Olga W. *The Novels of William Faulkner: A Critical Interpretation*. Baton Rouge: Louisiana State University Press, 1964.

Warren, Robert Penn. "Faulkner: The South and the Negro." *Southern Review*, n.s. 1 (1965): 501-29.

Wecter, Dixon. *Sam Clemens of Hannibal*. Boston: Houghton Mifflin Co., 1952.

Welty, Eudora. "Keela, the Outcast Indian Maiden." In *A Curtain of Green And Other Stories*. New York: Harcourt, Brace & World, 1936.

————. "Powerhouse." In *A Curtain of Green and Other Stories*. New York: Harcourt, Brace & World, 1936.

————. "A Worn Path." In *A Curtain of Green And Other Stories*. New York: Harcourt, Brace & World, 1936.

Whitman, Walt. *Leaves of Grass*. Comprehensive Reader's Edition. Edited by Harold W. Blodgett and Sculley Bradley. New York: New York University Press, 1965.

Wolfe, Thomas. *The Web and the Rock*. New York: Harper & Row, 1937.

Yellin, Jean Fagan. *The Intricate Knot: Black Figures in American Literature, 1776-1863*. New York: New York University Press, 1972.

Index

Adamowski, T. H., 103
Adventures of Huckleberry Finn, The
  (Clemens), 11 72, 86-96, 97, 108,
  116
Adventures of Tom Sawyer, The
  (Clemens), 72-85, 86, 110
American Dream, An (Mailer), 130,
  132
Anderson, John Q., 25, 27
"Artificial Nigger, The" (O'Connor),
  124-27, 130

Baldwin, Joseph G., 23-24
"Bear, The" (Faulkner), 102-3
"Benito Cereno" (Melville), 125
Bird, Robert Montgomery, 49-51
Birth of a Nation, The (Giffith), 7
"Black Prince, The" (Grau), 127-28
Blair, Walter, 19, 20, 25, 64, 75, 81
Blithedale Romance, The
  (Hawthorne), 126-27
Bodkin, Maud, 12
Brodwin, Stanley, 97
Brown, Sterling, 9
Browning, Preston M., Jr., 122

Caldwell, Erskine, 119
Cardwell, Guy A., 15, 40
Carringer, Robert L., 53
Cassique of Kiawah, The (Simms), 47
Cecil, L. Moffitt, 44
Censorship, in South, 39-40
Chase, Richard, 111

Civil War, influence in fiction, 15-16
Clansman, The (Dixon), 7-8
Cleaver, Eldridge, 105
Clemens, Samuel L., 17, 64, 72-100,
  108, 116, 122; *The Adventures of
  Huckleberry Finn*, 11, 72, 86-96,
  97, 108, 116; *The Adventures of
  Tom Sawyer*, 72-85, 86, 110; and
  Indian, 72-73; and Negro, 72-73;
  Pudd'nhead Wilson, 72, 86,
  97-100, 122; and racial
  stereotyping, 77 81, 83, 87, 90, 95;
  and science, 100; and sex
  stereotyping, 97-98, 99; and South,
  72-73
Comer, James P., 8-9
Cox, James M., 73, 87, 97, 98, 99
Cudjo's Cave (Trowbridge), 11
"Curious Widow, The" (Lewis),
  28-31, 37
Current-Garcia, Eugene, 64

Dabney, Lewis M., 102
"Delta Autumn" (Faulkner), 103
Depression, racial attitudes in, 17
Devin: archetype of, in literature,
  10-12; term for Indian, 10; term for
  Negro, 9-10; as variant of Shadow
  archetype, 9
DeVoto, Bernard, 73
Dixon, Thomas, Jr., 7-8, 16
Douglass, Frederick, 131
Doyno, Victor, 93

165